The Story of
Limbury-cum-Biscot

Colin R Cook

First published December 2007
By Colin R Cook in association with
The Book Castle,
12 Church Street,
Dunstable,
Bedfordshire
LU5 4RU

ISBN 978-0-9557010-0-9

Designed and typeset by Caroline and Roger Hillier
The Old Chapel Graphic Design
www.theoldchapelivinghoe.com

Printed by Antony Rowe Ltd., Chippenham, Wiltshire

Front cover picture:
Village of Biscot near Luton c 1815 (Thomas Fisher)
Bedfordshire & Luton Archives Service

The Prologue

This book traces the history of Limbury-cum-Biscot which up to the 1920s was a small village three miles to the north of Luton. Since that time Limbury-cum-Biscot has been absorbed into the Borough of Luton and now it is difficult to define its borders and special features.

There have been people living in the Limbury-cum-Biscot area since pre-history times and by the time of the Conquest it was a flourishing community. Biscot appears as a separate entry in the Domesday Book and was then valued at forty shillings, although previously its value was sixty shillings in Edward the Confessor's day.

The Moat House in the village is the oldest secular building in the Luton area and can be traced back to 1370–1400. It is now an attractive public house and restaurant.

John Sambrooke Crawley of Stockwood was the Lord of the Manor of Biscot and it was he who provided the land and the money for the building of Holy Trinity Church, Biscot which was completed in 1868.

This book, apart from following the development of Limbury-cum-Biscot over the years, gives a social insight of the village over the past 135 years through information obtained from parish archives, for which I thank the church authorities.

Acknowledgements

Thank you to Dr Elizabeth Adey of Luton Museums for all her time and help, to Dr James Dyer for his help in gaining copyright permission for some illustrations and also to Luton Reference Library. I am grateful to my wife for her help, advice, typing and checking spelling etc, and for reading through the finished book. Also thanks to the following for contributions to the book : Mrs Joyce Beetles; Dr James Dyer; Mr Ron Hudswell; Mr G J Horsler; Mrs Jessie Raymond; Mr Irving Rumbles; Mrs Mary Sanderson; Mr Roland Scanes; Dr Trevor Tween; Miss Mary Ward; Mr Williams – Methodist Archivist.

Illustrations

CC	Author
JGD	A History of Education in Luton – John G Dony
BLAS	Bedfordshire and Luton Archives Service
BSCB	Biscot Stewardship Campaign Book
JB	Mrs Joyce Beetles
KC	Mr Ken Cooper (Luton Scene Again)
GJH	The Deacons of Limbury Baptist Church
ME	Mr Michael Enticknap
AH	Mr A Hale (The Biscot Story)
AJ&MJH	A J & M J Hales
DK	Mr David Kingston (The Slip End Book)
EGM	Mr Eric G Meadows (Luton Past and Present)
JR	Mrs Jessie Raymond
LR	Mr Len Raymond
DTT	Dr Trevor Tween
PW	Mr Paul Welburn

Bibliography

History of Luton by Frederick Davis, 1855

History of Luton by William Austin, 1928

Memories of Biscot by Miss E D Smith, 1920s

The Biscot Story by A Hale, 1968

The Baptists of Limbury by G J Horsler, 1981

The Blockers' Seaside by C J Peaples, 1979

The Straw Trade by T G Austin, 1871

Contents

The Author

 The Author, Colin Cook, was born and brought up in Luton where he attended Tennyson Road Infants & Junior School and Surrey Street Secondary School. On leaving school Colin was apprenticed as a Fitter and Turner at Hayward Tyler & Co in Crawley Green Road, Luton. On completing his apprenticeship Colin gained employment in the Sales Office at Hayward Tyler where he worked until being made redundant in 1985. After this time he worked for other Pump Engineering Companies both in London and in Northfleet, Kent.

Colin has always been interested in industrial and social history and is a great collector of anything to do with this period in time and he has accumulated a huge collection of articles which he displays in five museums (sheds) in the back garden. Colin has researched and written about his interest and has given numerous talks on subjects such as "The Early Days of Hayward Tyler", "The Crawley Family Legacy in Luton", "Growing up during the War" and "A Walk to Biscot". Unfortunately, due to ill health, Colin has had to give up public speaking so he now concentrates on writing.

Colin married his wife, Gina, at Holy Trinity Church, Biscot, forty-one years ago and was churchwarden there for thirteen years. He has two sons, Peter, who works in Environmental Research, and Derek, a drama teacher and translator/interpreter, who lives in Sweden with his wife, Lotta, and their two children, Zoe and Elliot.

CHAPTER 1

Pre The Norman Conquest

eople have been living in the area around Biscot for thousands
of years. In the Stone and Bronze Ages trade in flint or in
finished axes came from the mines and family factories in what
we now call East Anglia. The trade flowed west and into the south east
along tracks, some of which were to become future major roads, for
example in our area the Icknield Way. By approximately 800BC traders
were bringing iron goods from Europe and iron was also starting to be
smelted in Britain.

The Icknield Way runs from the flint mines in Norfolk through
Cambridgeshire and Hertfordshire, Baldock and Letchworth following
approximately the A505, then over the ford at Ickleford and running to
the south of Pirton and to the north of Little Offley and on between
Deacons Hill and Markhams Hill and between Noon Hill and Telegraph
Hill (two miles north of Lilley).

The Way skirts round the north end of Luton, passing Warden Hills,
Galley Hill and Drays Ditches to the A6. It then follows closely the road
called Icknield Way, crossing the River Lea where the road changes its
name to Neville Road. At this point the Way probably follows a line to
Icknield Road on to Roman Road and Stoneygate Road, finally on to the
Dunstable Road (A505), the old Icknield Way into Dunstable where it
crosses the Watling Street. It then passes along the bottom of Dunstable
Downs and on to Ivinghoe Aston on the B489.

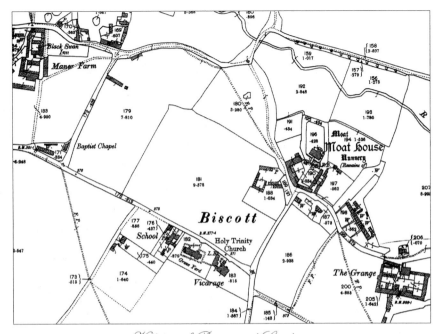

Villages of Biscot and Limbury

It is more than possible that such traders would have crossed the River Lea near to present Limbury-cum-Biscot, stopped to refresh themselves and carried out a little business, before proceeding on their way towards the Dunstable area. To the south of Biscot the ground rises to a ridge along which traders also came. The ridge was sometime called the Peddlers Way as were many other tracks across the country. Built on this ridge is believed to be a Neolithic barrow dating back to 2500BC and much later on this site was raised Biscot Mill. The ridge falls to the River Lea down the now Montrose Avenue, then rises steeply to Cowridge, Round Green and on to East Hyde.

Before the coming of the Romans, people of the Limbury-cum-Biscot area were part of the Catuvellauni tribe whose influence stretched from the north bank of the Thames up as far as Northamptonshire and approximately

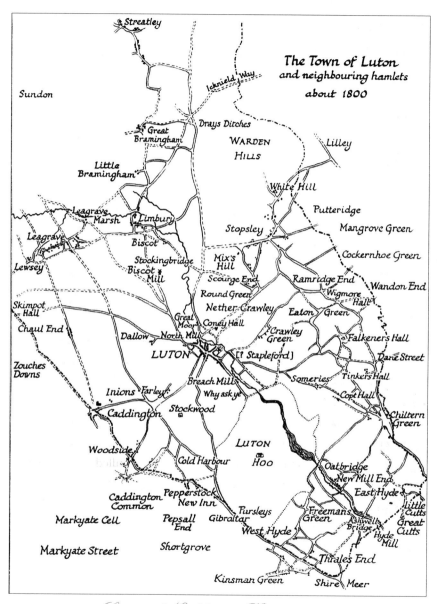

Streatley

The Town of Luton
and neighbouring hamlets
about 1800

Icknield Way

Sundon

Drays Ditches
Great
Bramingham   WARDEN   Lilley
HILLS
Little
Bramingham
White Hill

Leagrave   Putteridge
Marsh   Limbury
Leagrave   Stopsley   Mangrove Green
Biscot
Lewsey   Cockernhoe Green
Stockingbridge   Mix's
Biscot   Hill
Mill   Scourge End   Ramridge End
Round Green   Wigmore   Wandon End
Skimpot   Nether Crawley   Eaton   Green   Hall
Hall   Great   Coney Hall
Chaul End   Moor   Crawley
Dallow   North Mill   Green   Falkener's Hall
LUTON   [? Stapleford]   Dane Street
Zouches
Downs   Someries   Tinkers Hall
Inions Farley   Breach Mill
Why ask ye   Copt Hall
Caddington   Stockwood
Chiltern
Woodside   Green
Cold Harbour   LUTON
HOO
Caddington Pepperstock   Oatbridge
Common   New Inn   New Mill End
Pursleys   East Hyde   Little
Markyate Cell   Pepsall Gibraltar   Freemans   Cutts
End   Green   Ashwell   Great
West Hyde   Bridge   Hyde Cutts
Markyate Street   Shortgrove   Mill
Thrales End
Kinsman Green   Shire Meer

Luton and Neighbouring Hamlets (EGM)

3

from the Hertfordshire/Essex border across to Oxfordshire.

From 43AD onwards the people of a small settlement by the River Lea that was to become Biscot saw many Roman legions pass along the Icknield Way between Limbury-cum-Biscot and Durocobrivae (Dunstable). Roman settlements followed and, with the establishment of Verulamium (St Albans), many villas and farm houses were built in and about the now Luton area. Evidence of Roman occupation has been found at Leagrave, Limbury and Biscot and in other areas in Luton. The finds have been in the form of coins, pottery, middens, waste pits, burials and kilns. In 1906 a waste pit was found on Grange Farm at Biscot containing potsherds, human and animal bones, and refuse.

In the following four hundred years of Roman occupation the British tribes of the south east had become almost Romanised; the settlements at Limbury and Biscot took on a more regular way of life, for the Romans liked order and discipline, although inevitably this made inroads into personal freedoms. The Romans were great road builders and in our area built the Watling Street (now the A5), and where this road crosses the Icknield Way the town of Durocobrivae (Dunstable) was born.

In 410AD the Roman forces left Britain in order to defend their empire and eventually Rome itself from the hordes of invaders of Eastern Europe and Asia. The years of stability and order were coming to an end and Limbury-cum-Biscot like the whole of the country had again to learn how to defend themselves against invaders from all quarters looking to fill the power vacuum.

Early in the fifth century small groups of pagan Saxon mercenaries and their families had begun to settle in eastern England. Some made their home alongside the native Britons in the Upper Lea Valley. One group lived on the edge of the area and buried their dead in a cemetery that was discovered in 1925 on the hilltop between Biscot Mill and St Andrew's Church. The graves dated from the early fifth to late sixth centuries, and contained expensive jewellery and ceremonial weapons.

This was probably the beginning of permanent settlement in the Biscot -Limbury area.

In the year 571AD an army of West Saxons from Wessex carried out a series of raids along the Ridgeway and Icknield Way, attacking the townships of Benson, Eynsham, Aylesbury and Limbury, which enabled them to take control of much of the south Midlands. The attacks are recorded in the tenth century *Anglo-Saxon Chronicle* which tells us that the name Limbury was written *Lygeanbrig* at that time, meaning "the settlement on the river Lea". The Britons became a subject people and were gradually absorbed into the Saxon stock. As the Icknield Way was still the main roadway in the area it is probable that the site was fairly close to the River Lea, in fact in the vicinity of the present Biscot Church.

By the middle of the seventh century it is probable that the inhabitants of Lygeanbrig had become Christians, for in 653AD, Paeda, under-king of the middle Angles, had been baptised and had sent four priests to instruct his people in the new faith. One of these priests was the brother of Saint Chad called Cedd, who worked his way from Leicester into Bedfordshire. At this time the Luton area had been assigned to the diocese of Leicester. Christianity had now taken on such a fervour that Bede could say, "monasteries have become so numerous that no place can be found for the erection of others". From Cedd's ministry a small wooden church was built inside the settlement at Biscot. We do not know the fortunes of the settlement at Biscot, who its chief men were, nor even how big it was. At an early date the church and the land surrounding it became the property of a local monastery whose Abbott was called Alhmund. In 792AD King Offa of Mercia gave this same land, about 500 acres, to the first Abbott of Saint Albans. A house for the bishop of Mercia was built on the land at Biscot, so that the bishop would have somewhere to stay should he wish to visit that part of his large diocese. The name Bishopscote meaning Bishop's House (as dovecote means dove's house) still survives today in our name of Biscot and Bishopscote Road.

During the late seven hundreds the Vikings started their attacks on England and by 870AD they had conquered a large part of the country; only Wessex (West Saxon) remained in Saxon hands under Alfred the Great. After a battle between Alfred and the Danish Viking King Guthrum in 886AD a boundary between the two peoples was agreed, the line between them followed the rivers Thames, Lea, and Ouse (at that time the Lea was a much larger river) and a straight line between the Lea and Bedford. Luton was right on the boundary line. The settlements at Biscot and Limbury, together with the ones at Leagrave and Park Square Hill, were on the Saxon side of the river. There were unlikely to have been any border controls and therefore comings and goings and trade continued as before. A large proportion of the church land at Biscot was on the Danish side, and one of the effects of this partition was that the Abbey at Saint Albans lost the church at Biscot and its endowment. At about this time the town centre of Luton about Park Square appears to have developed and a church was erected on land claimed by the king.

Chiltern Hundreds

In the tenth century the English shires were the responsibility of the shire-reeve or sheriff (reeve is another name for magistrate). The shires were sub-divided into hundreds (a hundred ranged in area between 93 and 123 hides). In Bedfordshire there were nine whole hundreds and three half hundreds. Limbury-cum-Biscot was in the hundred called Flitt which stretched from Haynes and Clophill in the north to Caddington in the south. At this time the Flitt hundred did not include Luton, as Luton was royal land and the sheriff of Bedfordshire had no jurisdiction over royal lands of Luton, Houghton Regis and Leighton Buzzard. However by Mediaeval times Luton had been incorporated into the Flitt hundred and Leighton Buzzard into the hundred called Manshead.

In 913AD a party of Danish Vikings from Leicester and Northampton, so the Anglo Saxon Chronicle tells us, rode out against the settlements along the Lea, but the peoples of Limbury-cum-Biscot and the Lutonians put them to flight. By 975AD Luton was a royal town, as were Houghton Regis and Leighton Buzzard.

In 1013AD the Danish King Sweyn Forkbeard landed with his army in England and after a rapid campaign was accepted as king over most of the country, and was succeeded by his son Cnut in 1016AD.

Edward the Confessor became king in 1042AD, son of the Saxon King Aethelred II and Emma of Normandy. When Edward died in 1066AD he was succeeded by his brother-in-law Harold, although there was another contender for the English throne, William of Normandy. William had been promised the throne by Edward, and was not pleased to learn that Harold had been crowned king. Trouble was coming and the people of Limbury-cum-Biscot kept their heads down.

CHAPTER 2

After The Norman Conquest

*T*he Battle of Hastings, although involving only a comparatively small number of men on each side, was the most decisive single engagement in the history of our land. It lasted the whole of one day on the 14th October 1066 and ended with Harold slain and William conqueror of all England. Unfortunately no one appeared to take William's claim to the English throne seriously, perhaps due to the small number of men involved in the fighting; in any case he grew tired of waiting for the English lords to submit to him.

William took a roundabout route to London, the capital, testing all the time if there was any resistance to him; there was none. This, however, did not stop him from devastating the countryside, for the army was living off the land and this also meant impoverishing every village and town through which they passed, although the royal manors such as Luton were left untroubled. Luton may have escaped William's wrath but Biscot and Limbury were not so lucky, and it was many years before they recovered from the attacks made upon them. England's leaders finally submitted to William, and he was crowned king in Westminster Abbey on Christmas Day.

After William had secured the throne, one of his appointments was to make Ivo Taillebose, who was a Norman, sheriff of the royal manors of Luton and Houghton Regis. After Ivo had taken over the royal manors he found that smaller manors had grown up around them, which had been gifts of land from Edward the Confessor to people who had given him service. These smaller manors included that of Biscot. By 1086 the smaller manors had been added to the manor of Luton.

Also in 1086 William instructed that accounts be made of the whole country; these records formed the Domesday Book. The survey was very strictly adhered to and detailed every hide of land (one hide equals 120 acres approx.) and every animal, ox, cow and pig was counted, and how much tax the king should receive was calculated. Also included in the survey were the number of peasants (only men were counted, women and children excluded), ploughs, mills and the size of any woodlands. Biscot and Luton both appear in the Domesday Book as detailed overleaf. William died in 1087 after he had reigned for twenty one years and in this time had secured the Norman hold on the throne, stabilised the country and established a workable taxation based on the Domesday report.

Domesday at Biscot

Biscot has a separate mention in the Domesday Book and is described as follows:

Flictham Hundret

"Bissopescote was assessed at 5 hides T.R.E. (The Domesday rendering of T.R.E. was "In the year that King Edward was alive and was dead"). There is land for 5 ploughs. There are 2 ploughs on the demesne, and 10 villeins have 3 ploughs. There are 3 serfs and a meadow for 4 plough-teams. In all it is worth 40 shillings; when Ralph Taillebosc held it (was worth) the same amount; T.R.E. 60 shillings. This manor Edwin, a man of Ashgar, the staller, held and could do with it what ever he wished. Ralph Taillebosc added it to Loitone, (Luton) the king's manor, for the sake of the additional payment which it gave him; and separated it from the hundred in which it was assessed T.R.E. On the other hand he took other 5 hides from an other hundred and placed them in the Flictham Hundret."

Five kinds of peasants are recorded in the Domesday Book:

Freemen and Sokemen were bound to their lord by the paying of rent.

Villeins were subject to labour service to their lord and had a share of the common open field.

Cottars owned a small holding, but could be put to any kind of work that their lord decreed.

Slave or Serf was a chattel of his lord.

These categories are very fluid and could vary considerably from one part of the country to another.

Chronicle of Limbury-cum-Biscot

1086 Ivo Taillebose added Biscot to the Manor of Luton.

1100 William Rufus (The Red King) was disliked by all, but appears to have left Luton alone. He was succeeded by his brother Henry I.

1115 Henry, with his wife, was spending Christmas at St Albans with the Abbot Paul and during his visit made a grant to the abbey of the Manor of Biscot. This gift of the Manor of Biscot was originally made to the first Abbot of St Albans by King Offa when he founded the Abbey in the year 792AD. When granting Biscot to St Albans, Henry retained certain lands valued at 20 shillings, however they were sold to Paul's successor Abbot Geoffrey for one hundred grass oxen. In the records of this transaction Bishopscote is called for the first time by the abbreviated form of Biscote.

1145 In this year there was a nunnery at Markyate, which lay four miles from Luton. Mr Frederick Davis, in his "History of Luton", stated that a considerable house for nuns stood on the Moat Farm site at Biscot. However, Mr William Austin, in his "History of Luton" stated that there never was a nunnery at Biscot. It is, of course, possible that Davis was misled by Speed's list of Religious Houses in Bedfordshire. Speed referring to this nunnery states it was called "Holy Trinity de Bisco" when perhaps he should have written "Holy Trinity de Bosco" (in the wood).

Davis thought Bisco meant Biscot and placed the nunnery at Moat Farm. The nunnery at Markyate did, however, own some land at Leagrave about a mile from Moat Farm.

1199–1214 During this time John de Cella, Abbot of St Albans, gave ten librates of land in Biscot to Robert Fitz Walter, a man of great power and influence in the reign of King John. He was one of the barons appointed to hold the King to observance of the Great Charter, and after the sequestration of the property of Fitz Walter in 1216 it is probable that his interest in Biscot reverted to the Abbey.

1220 The church at Luton built a mission / parochial chapel at Limbury. In 1513 John Sylam, whose memorial is in St Mary's Church, left by will 6s 8d to the chapel at Limbury

1287 It was about this time that the Leper Hospital of St John was founded on the hills between Limbury and Leagrave in which lepers were isolated from the population. The existence of this Hospital of St John the Baptist was disclosed incidentally in the account of the lepers who in 1287 broke out of the Lazar House and entered Luton. It is worth recalling that leprosy in this country was stamped out by the church's insistence on the segregation of lepers and by building hospitals where they could live, fortified by the church's ministration, in isolation.

1289 At this time it seems that Hugh de Philibert held the Manor of Biscot as a tenant of the Abbey and that he granted his interest to William de Bereford

1370–1400 It is from this period that the current Moat House (farm) was originally built; parts of the original roof timbers are still preserved consisting of decorated arch-braced collar beams. It is this decoration which was thought too grand for a farm house, in fact more in keeping with a religious house.

1400–1548 The principal land owners at Biscot between 1289 and 1419 were the de Berefords, and between 1419 and 1548 the Acworths held that position. It seems probable that the de Berefords erected the original

Moat House which was modified by the Acworths.

1549 Biscot Manor was sold by the Acworths to a John Dermer.

1595 In this year by the foreclosure of a mortgage the manor became the property of Edward Wingate.

1597 Edward Wingate "Clerk of the Cheque of the Gard" held both the Manors of Biscot and Lewsey.

1605 George Wingate, Edward's nephew, also held both Biscot and Lewsey Manors.

1617 John (aged sixteen) succeeded his grandfather George to the above manors.

1675 John's son Francis Wingate held Biscot Manor and his brother George held Lewsey.

1691 Sir Francis Wingate, son of Francis, held Biscot Manor.

1718 Arthur, son of Sir Francis, held Biscot Manor and in 1724 sold the manor to John Crawley for £8,796.

1724 John Crawley sold his Someries estate and house to Sir John Napier, and went to live for a time in London and then in Harpenden, pending the building of Stockwood House in the neighbourhood where he had bought further land. The house was completed in 1740 and became the family home of the Crawleys well into the twentieth century.

1754 John Crawley made considerable additions to his property and now included both Moat and Grange Farms at Biscot.

1823 John Sambrooke Crawley, a descendant of the above, was born and became in due time Lord of the Manor of Biscot. He provided land and also the money for the building of a church in Biscot which was completed in 1868; he also provided a large vicarage which stood beside it. John Sambrooke Crawley financially supported many Anglican Churches in Luton and a number of Luton schools; his interests and help also extended to the building of the Cottage Hospital in High Town Road. John Sambrooke Crawley died on the 22nd September 1895 at Stockwood and was buried in St Andrew Churchyard, Woodside.

1855 The rapid rise in population in England in the nineteenth century including Luton and the surrounding area called for re-deployment of resources and an expansion of services and utilities. The Church of England was no exception, so the original parish of Luton was from 1855 onwards divided into smaller areas to provide new parishes and churches to serve the new urban populace.

1866 The parish of Biscot cum Limbury was formed in 1866 with the old manor as its focal point.

1868 The Lord of the Manor was John Sambrooke Crawley of Stockwood, who held the rectorial rights, which he made over for the endowment. He provided the land and the money for the building of the church, which was completed in 1868, and also for a very large vicarage which stood beside it.

A Deed dated 15th June 1866 stated that "John Sambrooke Crawley did give, grant, and convey to the Ecclesiastical Commissioners for England to and for the use of the minister for the time being of the district, certain tithes, or the tithe commutation rent charges, amounting together to the annual sum of £148 14s 3d, and issuing out of lands and hereditaments situate in the hamlet of Biscot cum Limbury, in the Parish of St. Mary, Luton; also a certain piece or parcel of land situate within the limits of the district hereinafter recommended to be constituted and containing 3 roods and 23½ perches or thereabouts, as and for the site of a church for the said intended district; also a certain other piece or parcel of land situate with in the limits of the said district containing 3 roods and 23½ perches or thereabouts, as and for a site for a parsonage or house of residence, with garden and glebe, for the minister for the time being for the same district, which district shall be called "The District of Biscot". The whole right of patronage of the said district so constituted be assigned to and be absolutely vested in, and shall and may be exercised by, the said John Sambrooke Crawley, his heirs and assigns for ever."

The following is the district of Biscot – "All that north-western part of the parish of St. Mary, Luton, in the county of Bedford and diocese of Ely, wherein the present incumbent of such parish now possesses the exclusive cure of souls, which now consists for the most part of the two hamlets of Leagrave and Biscot cum Limbury, and which is bounded on the west by the parishes of Toddington and Houghton Regis in the same county and diocese; on the north by the parishes of Streatley and Sundon in the same county and diocese; on the east by the district of Stopsley in the same county and diocese; and on the remaining side, that is on the south by the new parish of Christ Church, Luton, in the same county and diocese, and by the parish of Caddington, partly in the same county of Bedford and partly in the county of Hertford, and wholly in the said diocese of Ely."

CHAPTER 3

Memories of Biscot

J ust after the First World War, Miss E D Smith wrote a book called Memories of Biscot. She was the sister-in-law of the Rev Sidney H Collins, Vicar of Biscot, and stayed at the vicarage with him and her sister. The following is an excerpt from her book.

"It was All Hallows Eve, the 31st of October, a windy, star-lit night, with a full moon. I was coming from work, and had just got off the bus near Biscot, and was walking down Nunnery Lane, in no mind to hurry as my head was splitting with the incessant noise from the machinery at the factory. As I passed the Moat Farm, I remembered how the old pond, now filled in, used to shine in the moonlight, how the swallows dipped above it in the summer, and blue forget-me-nots grew beside it. And the chestnut tree since laid beneath the axe, dropped golden-bronze coloured leaves in the Autumn upon the pond's still waters: and how in Winter the children slid along its frozen surface. I missed the fine elms, stalwart and true comrades, near the roadside.

"My fancy took me back over a stretch of many years ... I saw the Saxon Earl, Edwin of Bishopscote, fair-skinned and strong-built, hunting the wild boar over the Biscot Common and through the woodlands. And I thought of the Priest named Morcar who owned woodlands of beech trees in Biscot which were sufficient to feed fifty swine, the pigs feeding on the nuts fallen from the trees. What a lovely sight it must have been in spring when the sun shone on the delicate green foliage of seventy-five acres of beech trees. How the ownership of fifty swine by a clergyman would be thought strange in these days. All this happened in Biscot before William the Conqueror landed in 1066 ... then part of his mighty army swept through Biscot on its way to Hertfordshire, and Morcar, the owner of the beech woodlands was taken prisoner: the countryside ravished, and then followed a terrible scarcity of food and much illness. My imagination pictured next the extremely proud knight, Philip de Limbury and Emma his haughty wife. This knight owned a mill at Limbury and was for ever quarrelling with his neighbours. There was one Robert Hull of Biscot, who claimed the right of digging turf to use for roofing his house, and also the cutting of bulrushes to clean the floors of his house. This right, Philip refused Robert Hull but was eventually silenced by the court at Bedford deciding in Robert's favour. At another time, he disputed some fishing rights along the banks of the river Lea, from Limbury Bridge to the Buttes. He also had terrible differences with the Abbot of St Alban's over that worthy's rights connected with Biscot and Limbury. (In 1115 Bishopscote had been granted by Henry I to the Abbot of St Alban's).

"One day in Luton, Philip came across the messenger sent by the Abbot to gather the dues. Philip promptly put him in the stocks. As a punishment for this offence, he had to take a large gift of money and lay it on the altar at St Albans. After his death, his widow Emma carried on his reputation by creating a feud over the right to reserve in Limbury Mead a pond covering some acres, as a fish stew, or a place for breeding fish.

"In contrast to Philip, I thought of Adam de Biscot who set out in 1247 to join the Friar Preachers, leaving all wealth and rank, bare-footed and poorly-clad, begging his bread and preaching the Gospel.

"In my mind I now see faces from Lorraine in France; these were straw-plaiters brought over by James I's mother Mary Stewart and taken by her to Scotland to begin the industry of plaiting. In Scotland they failed, and out of compassion James brought them to England where they settled in Luton and the surrounding area ... so in 1614 the fields were full of golden wheat, for the Bedford wheat straw was so much better for plaiting than the French.

"And then I saw a terrible time when Cromwell came, when fighting and arms became the work of most, although the Parliamentary forces met with little opposition round Biscot. However, Sir Francis Crawley in 1643 donned his armour against Cromwell on behalf of King Charles.

"At this point my eyes travelled to where the Biscot Mill stood, white in the moonlight. In our good Queen Bess's time it was working right merrily. In January 1841 a terrific thunderstorm broke over it, setting the mill alight, and burning it to the ground. However the mill was rebuilt, and has remained a welcome landmark for travellers for many a day."

A Census record gives us an insight of where people lived and how they made their living; examples from the 1881 Census give us the household record of two families living in Biscot.

Dwelling – Biscott Windmill

Household

George Gray	Head Married	Male	aged 38	Birthplace – Biscott	Miller	
Mary Gray	Wife Married	Female	aged 39	Birthplace – Barton	Straw Hat Sewer	
Sarah Gray	Daughter	Female	aged 17	Birthplace – Luton	Straw Hat Sewer	
Emily Gray	Daughter	Female	aged 16	Birthplace – Luton	Straw Hat Sewer	
Arthur Gray	Son	Male	aged 13	Birthplace – Luton	Scholar	
Florance Gray	Daughter	Female	aged 2	Birthplace – Biscott		
Anne Frost	Visitor	Female	aged 8	Birthplace – Barton		

Dwelling – Biscott

Household

David Bass	Head Married	Male	aged 46	Birthplace – Luton	Shepherd
Emma Bass	Wife Married	Female	aged 44	Birthplace – Biscott	Bonnet Sewer
Samuel Bass	Son	Male	aged 19	Birthplace – Biscott	Blocker
James Bass	Son	Male	aged 17	Birthplace – Biscott	Ag. Labourer
Jane Bass	Daughter	Female	aged 15	Birthplace – Biscott	Straw Machinist
Ada Bass	Daughter	Female	aged 14	Birthplace – Biscott	Straw Hat Sewer
John Bass	Son	Male	aged 11	Birthplace – Biscott	Ag. Labourer
Susannah Bass	Daughter	Female	aged 10	Birthplace – Biscott	Scholar
Charles Bass	Son	Male	aged 7	Birthplace – Biscott	Scholar
Emma Bass	Daughter	Female	aged 5	Birthplace – Biscott	Scholar
Mary Bass	Daughter	Female	aged 3	Birthplace – Biscott	
Maria Bass	Daughter	Female	aged 1	Birthplace – Biscott	

Biscot in 1915

Aubrey S Darby, author of "A View from the Alley", spent a convalescing holiday in Biscot recovering from a peritonitis operation carried out at the Bute Hospital. From his book I gather that the year was 1915 and Aubrey would have been ten years old. Aubrey's mother had a distant relative who lived in the village of Biscot and this seemed an ideal location to convalesce. Aubrey recalled Biscot as being a small hamlet, comprising two farms; Mr Craig farmed Moat Farm and Mr Hartops farmed Grange Farm. There was a pond in the road, a Parish church, a nearby school, and about fifty cottages mostly owned by the two farmers. The cottage where Aubrey stayed was in Moat Lane, one of a terraced row, and he recalled it was very small even when compared with his home in Princess Street. The cottage had no gas, electricity or piped water, the toilet being an earth closet thirty yards from the back door, and a communal well served the cottages.

The young man he stayed with was a farm labourer and his wife a housewife come washerwoman. There were no shops in Biscot at that time so the villagers had to provide for themselves, obtaining dairy products and eggs from the farm, becoming experts in cooking and providing game for the table. Aubrey experienced a healthy diet and good country air, and, as he said, this was not rural poverty, it was a rural paradise.

CHAPTER 4

Rural Industries

*E*ven up to the end of Victoria's reign, Limbury-cum-Biscot was still existing in splendid rural isolation. Farming was the main employer with Moat, Grange, and Limbury farms in the hamlets and flocks with shepherds on the hills.

We should not forget, however, that other industries flourished here; tanning, plaiting, reed cutting, together with farm related industries, milling, blacksmithing and wool-spinning in the home. I can find no mention of lace making, although this was practised in the north of the county.

Tanning

This was an activity carried out in Limbury as indicated in local nineteenth-century maps. Of all jobs that of the tanner must, because of the smells created, be the least popular. Tanners are mentioned in the Bible but the trade goes back much further than that. Because of its unsociable odours, tanneries were sited at the edge of a town or village, but due to the process requiring large amounts of water they were generally near a river or large stream, hence the position of Tanyard Cottage at Limbury.

The skins of cattle, horses, deer and sheep are used by the tanners in the manufacture of leather. The skins are immersed in vats, being first soaked in milk of lime for a few days, then washed until all trace of lime was removed. This softened the skin and the hair and much of the fat was scraped with a two handled tool like a large blunt spoke shave. After a few

Tanyard Cottage showing the Stokes sisters who lived there.

days in a very weak sulphuric acid to open the pores, they started their long journey through the pits of bark liquor. The first pit has weak, almost spent liquor, but successive pits were stronger until at last the hides were piled with fresh powdered bark between them, in a strong infusion of bark. At each pit the hides were regularly moved about and turned. The whole process took about a year.

From the above processes it is clear that a number of vats would be required in close proximity in the difficult handling of the skins, also the workers would require some form of weather protection. In view of this it is difficult to accept that the medieval fish stews at Limbury would have been used for tanning. Currently I have no information of how many workers were employed at the tanyard, but I suspect that at any one time it would not have exceeded a dozen.

The Hat Industry

Based on recent thinking straw plaiting was introduced into Great Britain by Lorrainers brought over from France by Mary Queen of Scots, although others suggest that straw plaiting was introduced by Flemish refugees, also in the mid-sixteenth century.

Why it should have concentrated in parts of Buckinghamshire, Hertfordshire and South Bedfordshire is not clear, but it may have had to do with the quality of the straw grown in this region. By the late seventeenth century it was well established as an important industry and it was calculated that nearly 1,000 families in Luton, Dunstable and the surrounding villages were solely dependent on the making of plait and straw hats. "A small neat manufactory of straw hats, baskets and toys" in Luton, Bedfordshire that maintains many of the poor, was observed by Thomas Pennant in 1782.

A large percentage of plait was made in the homes of the villagers where all the family were involved and Biscot, Limbury and Leagrave played their part. The plait produced by the villagers was sold, in rolls of 20 yards and in lengths called scores, to the plait dealers who visited the villages with their pony and carts. The rolls of plait were taken to the markets in the towns of Luton and Dunstable. Initially the dealers had stalls in the High Streets but later special plait halls were built.

Children were introduced to the industry at an early age by attending plaiting schools established at the beginning of the nineteenth century, or perhaps even earlier. The children were sent there as soon as they could walk and were set a task of plaiting a set number of yards by the parents. The schoolmistresses were often illiterate and some unable to plait, their task to see that the plait was made. They charged a weekly fee of 2d or 3d, and the children's earnings ranged from approximately 9d per week by the time they were eight up to 2s 6d at fourteen. The schools were held in cottages, the conditions were very poor and the rooms densely overcrowded: there are records of forty to sixty children in a room $10\frac{1}{2}$

Straw hat making in rural Luton (EGM)

feet square. Heating was by enclosed charcoal pots, as there was no room for a fire in such crowded conditions. Girls left when they were able to work steadily without constant supervision. Boys left when they were big enough to hold down other better paid jobs.

Plaiting was allowed in some parish schools for a part of the day in order to stimulate attendance. As late as 1874 there were in some local villages a number of plaiting schools but no day school. In 1875 the Luton School Board brought to court its first case for non-attendance at school, and from that time day school attendance increased and that of the plaiting schools decreased. As the plaiting schools were held in a room in a cottage, no trace of them can be found and we can only imagine with the help of drawings and reports what conditions were like.

Osier Beds in Limbury

Another rural industry carried out round and about Limbury-cum-Biscot was that of growing and harvesting the osier willow. The osier was not only used for the making of baskets but also for chair seats, cradles, baby pushchairs, sieves, eel traps and fencing.

The willow canes were bound together in bunches of approximately eighteen inches in diameter and seven to eight feet in length. One end would be levelled by a wooden bat. Various specimens of osier willow were grown in the beds with names such as Swallow Tail, Welch, Wheaton Gelster and Green Old Breed, each grown for particular applications. Sometimes many varieties were grown in the one bed.

The Luton Tithe Apportionment of 1844 details osier beds in the hamlet of Limbury-cum-Biscot as follows and detailed on the maps shown.

Map Ref No.	Land in Statute Measure			Occupier	Modern Location
	Acres	Roods	Poles		
290		1	8	James Kidman	Moat Farm Biscot
136		3	26	Thomas Partridge	Leagrave Marsh
150		1	16	Richard Stokes	Limbury Mead
239	1	1	37	William Ewer	Limbury
260			26	William Ewer	Limbury

Equivalents to measurements used above:

30 square Yards = One square Pole

40 square Poles = One Rood

4 Roods = One Acre

The soil for a new osier-bed was ploughed and cleaned as for any other crop. The cuttings or "sets" were placed in the ground in rows a few inches apart. The cuttings quickly took root and the bed was soon in full production.

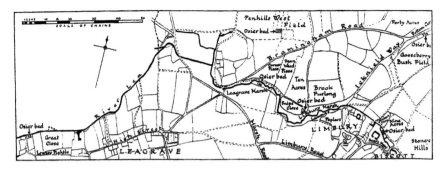

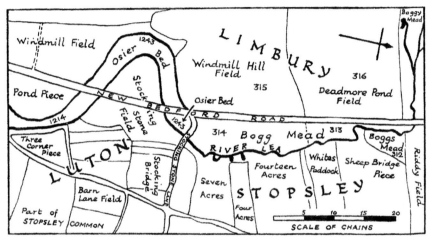

The osier beds from the map prepared for the Luton Tythe Apportionment 1844 detailing the area north of Luton (DTT)

The cutting usually took place when the leaves had fallen, about November time. The tools used for harvesting the osiers were poles similar to a boat hook for pulling bundles of willow to the bank, and knife or light hedge bill hooks for cutting, although for cutting the one year old osiers a short sickle was used. One and two year old osiers were sold for basket making, and the three year olds for fencing and general garden and farm use.

After being cut the osiers were tied into bundles until April time when peeling started. If it was warm and showery the rods would be ready for peeling much quicker in the season. Peeling and drying of the osiers was generally done by women for about six or seven weeks, finishing in time for hay making. The numbers of men involved in this seasonal work would normally be approximately two to three in an average size bed, however, when the osiers were ready for harvest the numbers would be supplemented by extra help from the farm. There were many basket makers to be supplied in the surrounding towns and villages, there being ten in Luton during the nineteenth century and three in Dunstable.

A fine collection of tools used by the osier cutters can be found in Stockwood Park Museum.

The osier beds and the cutters are now long gone, although the Lea still flows, and where there was once rural industry is now a County Wildlife Site. Luton Museums have published three excellent leaflets on Luton's Wetlands, the first following the River Lea from Midhurst Gardens to Fallowfield as it flows past Catches Field, Boggy Mead and River Close. An extract follows:

"Fallowfield is described as a secret place. As Luton spread out to enclose the lost hamlet of Biscot, these old meadows were almost forgotten. And of all the old habitats along the River Lea in Luton, they survive today as the best preserved. Many years ago Fallowfield was part of Biscot Grange Farm. The farm no longer exists, but older people can still remember shire horses grazing here after a long day's work at the local gravel pits".

The other leaflets relate to Cowslip Meadow or the Riddy, between the A6 and Springfield Road; and to Leagrave Common.

Many thanks to Dr Trevor Tween for allowing me to use extracts from Luton's Wetlands leaflets.

CHAPTER 5

Roads Around Biscot

Since the 1921 Survey of Luton a number of the roads around Biscot have changed their names, and many rural pathways have become major roads.

At the 1921 survey	Present day road names
Milton Road	Neville Road
Church Road	Trinity Road
Manor Road	The Close
Green Lane	Millfield Road
Path	Black Swan Lane
Path	Nunnery Lane
Path from Moat Farm to Grange Farm (Grange Farm was at the junction of Meadow Road and Moat Lane)	Moat Lane
Limbury Road (A continuation of Denbigh Road)	Bishopscote Road
Suggested Main Road	Austin Road (named after William Austin)
Suggested Main Road	St Margaret's Avenue & Bristol Road

CHAPTER 6

A Walk from Luton to Biscot

C ome with me now on a journey of the mind. It is the year 1890, there is a chilly wind this fine September afternoon as we start a walk to Biscot. We are starting from George Street, Luton and make our way past horse drawn carts laden with hat boxes taking hats from the factories down Bute Street and on to the railway stations.

Our walk takes us down Manchester Street, formerly called Tower Hill, and into the aristocratic area of New Bedford Road, and then across

Biscot Windmill (KC)

Biscot Windmill (KC)

the Great Moor where we pick up the lane to Biscot (later called Biscot Road) and soon are at the end of the row of houses on the outskirts of the north side of the town of Luton. The lane gently rises so that you may see the New Bedford Road below and the Bramingham Shott estate, later to be called Wardown. This will be a perfect park for a people's playground, well wooded and easily accessible, but some way from the town. The lane now becomes a path between arable fields, and passing a large corn-rick, we see farmhands gathering the remaining bunches of corn and a little beyond, a farmer's cart ready to convey their burdens to the rick. In the distance, on the ridge, stands Biscot Windmill, keeping watch over fields looking somewhat bleak in the watery sun. We do not know how long ago it was when the first mill stood on this site but the pasture on which it stands is known as Mill Field (Millfield Road).

From the ridge the land to the east falls gently down to the River Lea at a spot called Stockingstone (the boundary between the parishes of Biscot and Stopsley); the ground then rises steeply to Cowridge and on to Round Green. Our way is north down a steep path (now called St Margarets Avenue) to the right of the mill down to the village of Biscot nestling under the lee of the ridge. The path once called Limbury Road is now Bishopscote Road. On entering the village we follow a large imposing wall which encloses the gardens and vicarage of Holy Trinity Church and follow the wall into Church Road (now Trinity Road) and note the sweeping entrance to the imposing vicarage.

The stables, incorporating horses and carriages built at the same time as the church and vicarage, are to our right, separating the vicarage from the churchyard. We would have been drawn to the stables by the sound of a whistling young stable lad at work sweeping the hay. We watch him at work, when he suddenly stops whistling and looks directly at us; he senses something is there, but we are from the future and he can not see us. After a minute or so he smiles to himself and continues with his work but the whistling is not so carefree.

(This building with modifications is the current church hall. The original door to the hay loft can still be seen above our heads. The hay loft would possibly have housed the stable lad. In later times it became a den for the youth club. The stables had windows much smaller than those seen today, and therefore a fan-light was placed in the roof; this has always been a problem with rain water finding a way in, and causing difficulty in darkening the room for slide shows.

At the outbreak of the Second World War the parish room which stood between the vicarage and the stables was converted into an A R P First Aid Post. Part of the stables became a garage for ambulances and Civil Defence vehicles, the remainder converted into a school canteen. The Parish Institute, which once stood on the church car park site, was used during the war by the London County Council for evacuee school children and also as part of the Sunday School for the church.

In 1956 it was decided to demolish part of the vicarage, which included the butler's pantry, the scullery, the coals and harness rooms, with the parish room converted into a garage for the vicar. At this time a church hall was proposed using the old school canteen and the old garage. The garage was changed into a vestibule and a porch created. A store room and toilet block was built together with a boiler room on the side of the old garage entrance and part of the school canteen. The old school canteen was extended to include a hall stage and dressing rooms, and a separate kitchen was built.)

Walking past we come to Biscot Church, which is dedicated to the Holy Trinity, the church and vicarage built by the Lord of the Manor of Biscot, John Sambrooke Crawley of Stockwood in 1868. The church is a pleasant and restrained example in the general trend of its day, when Gothic revival in the Early English Style was fashionable for ecclesiastical and school buildings. The use of bricks and stonework of contrasting colours was a characteristic of this architecture, as is exemplified by George Gilbert Scott's St Pancras Hotel which was being built at this time. It is interesting to note that the Leicestershire red sandstone used in the string courses and plinth in Biscot Church is the same as in that building. The building of the Midland Railway, commenced some four years before, had facilitated in the transport of this material.

At the side of the Churchyard is a neat gothic primary school erected by Luton School Board with separate accommodation for the headmaster.

We retrace our steps to the centre of Biscot Village and walk down Nunnery Lane, and would have passed the village pond and the large tithe barn arriving at Moat Farm (now The Old Moat House Restaurant).

After leaving Moat Farm we walk down a path called Moat Lane passing two rows of terraced houses occupied by farm workers, and on to Meadow Lane where used to stand Grange Farm. The day is now nearly spent, so we make our way past Biscot Church and on to Limbury with

Two attractive rows of terraced cottages in Moat Lane. These date back to the mid-nineteenth century and were originally for farm labourers working at Moat and Grange Farms. (CC)

its attractive Baptist Chapel and Black Swan Inn. Leagrave, with its rail station, is now in our sights and, as the train takes us back to Luton, we could look across to Holy Trinity Church and make a note to return in the not too distant future.

CHAPTER 7

The Biscot Windmill

*I*n the early nineteenth century Luton was served by water mills; North Mill which was later to give Mill Street its name, Brache Mill off the now Osbourne Road and Hyde Mill on the south side of Luton Hoo. There were also windmills; Rye Mill at the top of Cromwell Hill, and one near Villa Road. In High Town there was a mill near Welbeck Road (originally called Windmill Street), also another

Biscot Windmill (KC)

Biscot Windmill (PW)

stood by Windmill Road. Outside Luton to the north was Biscot Mill serving the villages of Biscot, Limbury and Leagrave.

The village of Biscot had a windmill for over 400 years, the first one being a post mill which stood in Windmill Field (near Millfield Road). When a new lease for the mill was drawn up in 1710 it belonged to Lady Ann Windgate of Toddington, and from the documents the tenancy was taken by Isaac Freeman of Biscot, miller. The deed recites that an ancient windmill had stood on the site and that Freeman and his successors were to rebuild the mill and keep it in good repair; the tenancy was for 500 years at a rent of sixpence per year. This was dissolved when the mill was struck by lightning in 1841 and burnt to the ground.

In a further deed dated 7th August 1855, it was recited that the mill had been destroyed by fire and had been rebuilt three years later as a smock mill, and was by the said deed vested in William Drewett, baker of Park Street, Luton. The last owner was Mr A H Tooley who in 1926 removed the sails and milled by an electric motor. The smock gradually deteriorated and was dismantled in 1938.

CHAPTER 8

The Moat House at Biscot

After leaving Biscot Church we cross Trinity Road (previously called Church Road) and make our way down Nunnery Lane. In front of us where Nunnery Lane meets Moat Lane we would have seen the tithe barn and village pond, and also farm outhouses. These have now been demolished, leaving only Moat House Farm which is now known as the Old Moat House, the oldest secular building in Luton, built sometime between 1370 and 1400. It is now a public house and restaurant.

The Moat House was a manor house up to the end of the seventeenth century and then continued in occupation as a farm house through the eighteenth and nineteenth centuries. It ceased to be inhabited in 1958 and its future became a matter of doubt and concern for those who care for local history.

After being acquired by Bedfordshire Council, with its preservation in mind it passed to the care of Luton Corporation on attainment of Country Borough status. For the next few years it suffered considerably from vandal damage, including two fires and from the effects of neglect and decay. From the early 1970s its fortunes changed dramatically and it is now a very popular meeting place restored to its former glory with a few sympathetic modifications.

Holy Trinity Church has a tangible connection with the Moat House in the shape of two iron chests which were found buried on the farm

The Moat House showing Totternhoe stone buttresses (EGM)

shortly after 1850. The land belonging as it did to Squire Crawley, they passed into his possession. One of the chests is now in Biscot Church and the other at Stockwood Museum. The chests which date from the early seventeenth century were perhaps intended as deed boxes.

The original purpose of the Moat House has been the subject of some controversy over the years. Historians disputing over the roofing beams, which are of oak and of great strength, richly moulded, perhaps a bit too fancy for a manor or farm house. This has led some to believe that this was a chapel roof, as writings state "There was formerly a considerable house for Nuns at Biscot founded by Roger, Abbot of St Albans, and dedicated to the Holy Trinity".

Frederick Davis in his "History of Luton" 1874 states "At its dissolution this religious house was valued at £143 18s 3d". There are some portions of the original building still standing which now form part of the restaurant. It must have been a place of great strength and extent, as the walls still standing are very thick. At one end of the house are two strong buttresses of Totternhoe stone, evidently part of the original building. Some of the chimney pieces still remain, which are massive and built of the same stone. On one of the chimney pieces, deeply cut in capitals, is the following: "There was hailstons fel 23rd July of this bignes and liknes – 1666. TF." One of the stones was circular, and measured no less than half an inch in diameter, the other was oval, and measured one inch in length.

In all parts of the garden adjoining the House are the remains of strong foundations. A moat surrounds the site, and on the north side there are signs of a former drawbridge. Existing roads and approaches show that the original main entrance is where it is now on the south of the island.

William Austin's "History of Luton" 1928 states that the Moat House was not a religious house but an extremely fine manor house. Mr Frederick G Gurney in a letter to William Austin says of the Moat House: "The larger half of the building remained as an open hall until the end or soon after the end of the 15th century, when the fine roof was added. The dividing up into rooms and floors seems mainly 17th century work, but may belong to the end of the 16th.

"The quadrangle of accessory buildings, kitchen, stables, threshing-floor and the like, stood north of the House and within the moat. The out-buildings seem to have been no older than the 17th century. To whom are we to attribute the erection of this House? The principal land owners at Biscot between 1289 and 1400 were the de Berefords and between 1400 and 1548 the Acworths. It seems probable therefore that a de Bereford

Inscription in the Moat House cellar (EGM)

erected the original house and that it was in parts rebuilt and enlarged by the Acworths."

A floor tile found on the site in 1981, probably a church tile, the fine open roof and the collar beams which have been brought to the house after the dissolution of the monasteries in the sixteenth century, could bear out the fact that the Moat House was at one time used as a religious meeting place.

The building continued in occupation as a farm house during the eighteenth and nineteenth centuries. It was at this time that country fairs were regularly held on the land immediately to the west of the site and later the dray horses from Luton's hat factories and breweries were brought out of the town to graze on Fallowfield which lies to the east, as its marshy land was beneficial to their hooves. The old farm-workers'

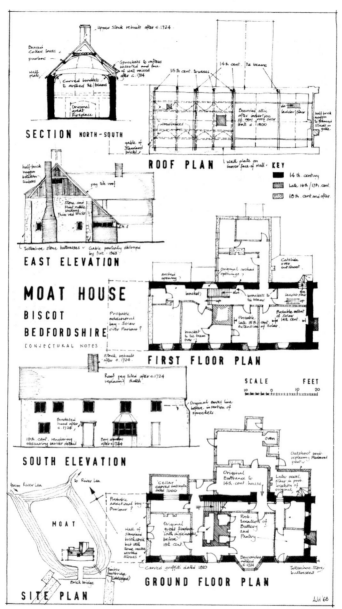

Plan of the Moat House at the time of its refurbishment in the early 1960s incorporating details dating from the fourteenth century (AJ&MJH)

Roof in the Moat House dining room (EGM)

cottages still stand in Moat Lane. There are many reports of a veiled spirit which has been sighted roaming the lands in the near vicinity.

Were there nuns in Biscot? I can only say that on dark foggy winters' evenings you may still see black hooded figures hurrying along Nunnery Lane responding to the distant ring of a church bell. I was told of nun-like ghostly figures being seen in the front rooms of houses in the lane. Some residents have now moved.

From maps of the villages of Biscot and Limbury before the encroachment of Luton, a number of small ponds are indicated just to the north of Black Swan Lane between the now Riverside Road and Runfold Avenue. These have been identified as medieval fish stews (ponds), used as a food source in winter for Limbury Manor or Biscot Moat House. Later these ponds could well have been used as tanning pits, for they are sited

The Moat House as a restaurant (EGM)

not far from Tanyard Cottage, Limbury, which was close to Riverside Road and the river.

Also in the same area between Black Swan Lane and the river, to the east of Runfold Avenue, there was once a sizeable square plot of land surrounded by a moat, which had an entrance to the south. This was known as Bears Moat, but its use remains a mystery. Perhaps it was an elaborate cattle pen.

CHAPTER 9

Limbury Manor

*W*hilst on holiday in Felixstowe we met by chance in the hotel where we were staying a Mrs Joyce Beetles, who was also on holiday and during our conversations mentioned that she was born in Luton in the 1920s. It also transpired that her grandfather at one time owned Limbury Manor.

View of Limbury Manor in the 1920s (JB)

Joyce Beetle's grandfather's family at Limbury Manor (JB)

I told Joyce that this was an extraordinary piece of luck as I was writing a book "Limbury-cum-Biscot" and currently seeking further information regarding Limbury Manor. Joyce recalls from the age of six years visiting Luton and staying at Limbury Manor and that there were on the ground floor, apart from the usual kitchen, dining and reception rooms, a Chinese room and a billiard room. Joyce's grandfather was Oliver Henry Edwards who died in 1943, aged seventy-nine years and was buried in Biscot Churchyard (Grave Plot F 1.18).

Since we have returned home Joyce's son has kindly sent to me photographs of the manor from that time which enabled me to fill in a number of gaps in my data.

From the photographs it would appear that the manor was built in the early part of the nineteenth century. During the 1920s it was a family home, one of the photographs showing Mr Edwards' second wife and their children. Joyce also spoke of the River Lea being at the bottom of the manor gardens. However, as it stood on the opposite side of the road from the Black Swan Inn this would seem incorrect.

I showed these photographs to a friend, a Mr Ronald Hudswell, who has lived in the Limbury area since the 1950s, and he was able to identify and confirm the location of the manor, and also the roof of the old tannery cottage just across the river, home for a time of the Stoke sisters.

Ronald also told me that his stepfather's aunt, Harriet Jane Potts, was in service at the manor in the early 1900s, starting work there from school at the tender age of thirteen years. At that time she was living at Slip End, a village on the other side of Stockwood Park, where her father was the village blacksmith, and would walk to Limbury Manor early on Monday morning, returning home on Friday evening. Harriet worked at the manor until she was in her mid twenties when she married Joe O'Dell, a local Slip End lad.

The manor was demolished in 1964 and now a block of flats occupies the site.

CHAPTER 10

Religion and Education

*I*n the thirteenth century St Mary's was the only church serving Luton and the surrounding hamlets, although there had been chapels in private mansions and hospitals since the Conquest. However in 1282 the Statutes of Winchester stated that mission or parochial chapels with graveyards were to be built in all hamlets more than two miles from the parish church.

Limbury was one of the oldest hamlets around Luton and had its own parochial chapel close to where Leagrave Junior School now stands. Record is made that Richard, son of Baldwin, had been appointed to the church at Limbury in 1220. The main church festivals gave the common people a chance to enjoy themselves, and at Limbury Chapel people from the surrounding area met in 1247 for a sports day. On this day there was a scuffle and William who came from Houghton Regis shot Roger le Keu with an arrow and fled; the people from Biscot and Limbury were fined because they did not seize him.

By the nineteenth century the chapel at Limbury had disappeared and to attend church or any of the non-conformist chapels meant a walk to Luton; the same was true with regard to schooling.

However by 1845 as per Frederick Davis the Luton historian, the Wesleyan Methodists had built a neat chapel at Limbury which will seat 100 persons, at a cost of £300.00 including the ground. By 1884 there were thirty-six children attending the Sunday School with eight teachers.

The chapel continued to serve the people of Limbury-cum-Biscot up until 1893 and was demolished in the early 1900s. The chapel stood in Neville Road at the junction with Neville Passage opposite Rose Villa. Rose Villa still stands today (July 2005) on the corner of Neville Road and Neville Passage, but it is in poor condition. It is interesting to note that a house which once stood at number 12 Neville Road was called Wesley Cottage. A second Methodist church was proposed in 1913 located at Norton Road with 300 seats at an approximate cost of £1,100.00. This project did not proceed and the funds went on buying land near the Biscot Mill for the building of St Margaret's Church. (From information kindly given by Mr Irving Rumbles Methodist, Circuit Archivist, and Mr Williams).

Although Biscot and Limbury were small hamlets two miles to the north of Luton, the influence of the Baptists from Park Street was also in evidence. Daniel Gutteridge of Biscot was a regular subscriber to the Park Street Church and his name appears on the list of Trustees in 1789 and again in 1807. He died in 1829 and his property and land were put up for auction, which included Limbury Manor Farm (the Manor House was demolished in 1964, and stood between Black Swan Lane and The Close). The Manor House was brought by Edmund Waller of Luton, who was a hat manufacturer and a prominent member of the Park Street Church, being a Trustee in 1829. Daniel Gutteridge's other farm at Limbury was bought by William Ewer of Lilley who lived for sometime in Limbury, and was also a Trustee at Park Street Baptist Church in 1829. The Baptists therefore were strongly represented in the Biscot and Limbury area by influential members of the church in Park Street.

From the second decade of the century services were starting to be held by members of Park Street at Limbury led by the minister, the Rev Ebenezer Daniel (minister from 1811 to 1830) being the first to attempt work there. Cottage meetings were held regularly by Rev E Daniel and continued for some time by the Rev Henry Burgess who succeeded him as minister. Then for some reason the services were discontinued until

September 1838 when Mr James William Menlove, the Town Missionary from the Luton Parish Church, commenced visiting Biscot and Limbury.

James Menlove was the son of the head gardener employed by Mr Burr of Luton and was later to take over from his father, gaining the love and respect of the family. Outside of work, as he grew older, he was often found reading the Bible to the poor in the Old Yard or St Ann's Lane, commencing the work he was to fulfil as a Town Missionary. This work included a variety of duties. Besides visiting the sick, he held Cottage meetings in various parts of the town and in the villages of Stopsley, Round Green, Limbury, Biscot, Caddington, Pepperstock and Kingsbourne Green. He also visited the Union Infirmary and the Hospital. He was well fitted for this work, often being told by the people that they could speak to him freely.

James Menlove succeeded in forming a Sunday School at Biscot and it is most interesting that this was a united effort, both Church and Non-Conformist parents sending their children for instruction, and children also came from Limbury and Leagrave. This led to Sunday evening services conducted by Mr Menlove and attended by all sections of the Christian church, these services being held in a cottage at Biscot.

The Vicar of Luton, the Rev Thomas Bartlett and Mr John S Crawley, Lord of the Manor of Biscot, at this time (1855) erected a schoolroom and cottage for a National Day School at Biscot and allowed James Menlove the use of the schoolroom for Sunday services, which continued for a number of years with increased membership.

A religious census taken in March 1851 produced the following statement signed by the Rev J Jordan Davies, minister of Park Street Church, Luton:

Limbury Baptists – House occupied by Mr Cumberland

Sittings – 56

General Congregation evening – 26

Average for preceding six months – 50

Village Station connected with Old Meeting House, Luton

The work at Biscot and Limbury had a profound effect on James
Menlove and, after reading Mr Spurgeon's sermon on baptism and much
prayer, he was led to become a member of the Baptist Church. He was
baptised on the Sunday, 2nd July 1865 at Park Street Church.

For a further twelve months Mr Menlove was allowed to continue at
Biscot and Limbury as Town Missionary, not withstanding his membership
at Park Street, because as he said the Vicar of Luton had no one to take
his place. He then received a letter from Mr J S Crawley stating that a new
parish had been formed which included the hamlets of Biscot, Limbury
and Leagrave, and that the Rev E R Adams had been appointed Vicar.
This was a great blow to the Baptists at Biscot and Limbury and caused
a rift between them and their Anglican brothers after years of a unified
community in the Biscot area.

The Baptists endeavoured to obtain a cottage at Biscot, but without any
joy. However Mrs H Stokes, who lived at a cottage known as "Tanyard"
in Limbury, near the river and between the present Neville and Riverside
Roads, offered her house for services and here the first Baptist Sunday
School was formed. The workers at the first meeting of the school were
Mr Menlove, Mrs Hannah Stokes and Mrs Hannah Bass, together with
nine scholars. Other church members opened their homes for meetings
and services including William and Emma Horsler who opened their
cottage at Biscot. This cottage had stood by the bank of the River Lea,
in the area between Runfold Avenue and Neville Road and at the end
of what is now Riverside Way, since at least 1840. There had been a
small tannery where Neville Road crosses the river and this house was the
tanner's home. Before the Baptist Chapel in Kingsley Road was opened
in 1868, meetings for the congregation were held in this house for around
two years. The house was demolished during the 1930s.

For eighteen months the little church worshipped in Mrs Stokes' house
with the congregations increasing, and a cottage was taken in Limbury
until a Chapel could be erected. Great difficulties were encountered

Old Limbury Baptist Chapel in Neville Road 1868 (GJH)

Old Limbury Baptist Chapel converted into modern day residential dwelling (CC)

before a site could be procured, as no-one was willing to sell them ground for such a purpose. Mr John S. Crawley owned most of the land in the Biscot area and Mrs Eliza Waller held the Limbury Manor Estate, but there was however some land in Limbury still held by the sons of William Ewer. A plot, situated between what we know as Trinity and Kingsley Roads, was admirably suited as a site for the church. Mrs Hannah Stokes walked from Limbury to Lilley and obtained from William and Daniel Ewer a promise to let the Limbury Baptists have a part of this plot of land. They also gave Mrs Stokes permission to proceed and build without delay.

For an outlay of £15, the cost of the site, the Limbury Baptist Church had a home of its own. The chapel opened for worship on Good Friday 1868 just before Holy Trinity Church at Biscot, which opened on Trinity

Limbury Baptist Chapel — present day (CC)

Sunday. Mr Barton was appointed superintendent, followed by Mr D Pike and Mr J Menlove in 1870. The work prospered and the chapel was enlarged in 1881.

We are fortunate in having an insight into James Menlove's domestic life which was a trying one and which made him more able to sympathise with others' afflictions. He was married in 1853 to a devoted Christian woman, but unfortunately one not in good health, who, after twenty two weeks of patient suffering, died of consumption in April 1868. Two of their children also died of consumption, one aged thirteen, the other aged fourteen. James married his second wife in September 1869 but was also bereaved of her in November 1873. He then married his third wife in May 1875 who survived him. James Menlove passed away on 15th July 1886.

This chapter is an extract from Mr G J Horsler's book "The Baptists of Limbury" for which I acknowledge with thanks permission given by the Rev P Hartnell and Limbury Baptist Church.

CHAPTER 11

Schools in Biscot

When Victoria came to the throne in 1837, education of the poor was still considered by many to be both unnecessary and possibly dangerous. James Kay-Shuttleworth, an assistant Poor Law Commissioner, stated in 1838 that "The state had the responsibility of rearing children in religion and industry, and to give them sufficient secular education as may fit them to discharge the duties of their station." The aim was to enforce such social discipline that would fit working class children to the needs of an increasing mechanical society.

Schools even up to the end of the nineteenth century had to compete with work for the child's time, and tensions arose between sending them to school or to work. One solution was to make use of the one day of the week when children's labour was not required – Sunday. From the late eighteenth century children poured into Sunday schools where a basic education was given and by 1850 over two million working class children were enrolled.

In the eighteenth century great strides had been made in the provision of charity (non fee paying) schools; in Victorian times voluntary efforts to overcome social problems including education of the poor was the norm.

In 1803 Joseph Lancaster published a book "Improvements in Education"; he believed that teachers should be selected and trained. He had opened his school in Borough Road, London in 1801; the best scholars were made monitors and each was put in charge of a small number of pupils. Lancaster taught the monitors at the start of each day before the other children arrived. Later on the monitors taught the pupils in their different groups.

From Lancaster's book "The whole school is arranged in classes; a monitor is appointed to each, who is responsible for the cleanliness, order and improvement of every boy in it. The proportion of boys who teach, either in reading, writing or arithmetic, is one in ten." All over the world people were searching for ways to teach children Quickly, Economically and Efficiently; the Lancastrian Monitorial System seemed to fill this need.

In 1808 the Royal Lancastrian Society was set up by the non-conformist supporters of Joseph Lancaster, and it was re-formed in 1814 as the British and Foreign Schools Society. The Church of England in 1811 formed the National Society for Promoting the Education of the Poor in the Principles of the Established Church. Andrew Bell the champion of the Anglicans also claimed to have invented the monitorial system, and both societies built schools throughout England. Most of the country had voluntary schools of one description or another and many of their former buildings are still in use today.

At this stage fees were levelled against each child attending the schools which varied from area to area from 2d to 6d per week, though for those in great need the fees were sometimes waived. It was not uncommon for the brightest child only to be sent to school who would then come home to teach the rest. On the other hand, by paying a little more a child would receive special attention. Because of the fee paying system children started school at any age between six and ten years, some stopping only for one year, while others would take one or two years out before returning to their studies, as the parents' finances fluctuated. This put a great strain on the teachers and the teaching monitors, some of whom were only eight or nine years old.

At first the voluntary schools were self-financing, but in 1833 the government voted a building grant of £20,000 per year; however, sums would only be paid when a least half the cost had been raised by private subscription. In 1839 a government committee was established to oversee elementary education; a body of Her Majesty's Inspectors was appointed and grant aid placed on a more regular footing. Minimum floor areas were laid down, fluctuating between six and ten square feet per child.

It was becoming clear that the government would have to do more than provide funds to subsidise voluntary effort if the needs of the whole country were to be met. It was not until the Educational Act of 1870 that a way forward was established. This Act called for Local Councils to set up School Boards which would provide additional schools in order that all children would have access to a primary education. Rate aid to the school boards meant that the schools of the new local authorities could be built on a scale and to a standard which the voluntary societies found difficult to match. School Boards did not have the power to provide secondary schools, nor did it advance the establishment of a connection between primary and secondary education.

In 1880 school attendance became obligatory for all children between five and ten years. This was raised to twelve years in 1899.

In 1890 primary school fees were abolished in most schools; all primary school fees were abolished in 1918.

By 1902 the created School Boards proved to be too small to deal with higher education, and the voluntary schools, British and National, were labouring under increasing difficulties. The Balfour Education Act of this date decided that the School Boards and the Voluntary schools should go and education, both primary and secondary, placed under the control of the newly created county councils and county boroughs. This is still the basis of the English educational system today. The School Boards objected to the changes but to no avail and they passed into education history.

The official school leaving age was now set at thirteen years; however the need for labour on the land, in service and in industry, especially during the First World War, became a matter of government concern. Boys, and in many cases girls, could obtain a School Leavers Certificate enabling them to leave school at the age of twelve years, providing work was available and that they could pass a leavers examination, demonstrating they had reached a certain standard of education.

Research to date indicates that there have been three schools in Biscot.

The first was a small Church of England National Day School for fifty children which was established in 1855 in connection with Luton Parish Church. The schoolroom, with teacher's residence attached, was built at the expense of John S Crawley Esq, of Stockwood. There was is also a Church Sunday School held here. The location of this school is given by a number of sources as by the Biscot Mill. John S Crawley Esq, who was Lord of the Manor of Stopsley as well as Biscot, also erected upon a piece of waste land at Stopsley, at his own expense, a National School for the accommodation of 200 children, with a neat building attached for the master. This school measured 50 feet by 20 feet. In 1871 John Crawley appears to have surrendered his school managementship, and the next year Biscot School closed. In the same year it was reported that an accommodation for seventy-eight children was required at Biscot and a further eighty at Leagrave. A schools inspector Mr C E Johnstone sent to Luton to report on the overcrowding of schools in the area, stated that the appointment of a certified teacher could save the situation. Events overtook this possible solution when the school at Biscot was demolished by its proprietors in the same year as its closure.

From Jacqueline Day's History of Education 1874–1883, the proportion of children receiving education in the hamlets to the north of Luton in 1874 were as follows:

Area	Age	Receiving Education	Not Receiving Education
Limbury/ Biscot	0–13	Boys 15 Girls 20	Boys 47 Girls 52
Leagrave	0–13	Boys 19 Girls 13	Boys 39 Girls 42

Source: T G Austin – The Straw Trade 1871

At this time, from the accounts of Holy Trinity Church Biscot for 1870 and 1871, funds were being raised for a school at Leagrave, although it was not until 1876 that a Board School was built.

From 1872 the Vicar of Biscot, the Rev E R Adams, was then faced with a parish which included Limbury and Leagrave with 887 inhabitants having no school to send their children. There was no probability of such accommodation being provided otherwise than by the formation of a School Board. The Vicar of Luton, the Rev J O'Neill, who was against the School Board, had suggested that the children could walk the three miles into Luton. The election for a School Board took place in Luton on 17th February 1874; those in favour were the Liberal Non-Conformists, against were the Conservative Anglicans. Adams, with the promise of a school at Biscot, sided with the Non-Conformists who won the day.

It would be another two years before a Board School was built at Biscot, in the meantime Adams had made temporary arrangements at Biscot. From the 1872 Church Accounts Rev Adams rented Mission Cottage and installed school furniture; the rent of the cottage for the year 1872 and the cost of the furniture amounted to £4-14-8d. A schoolmistress was engaged and from Church Accounts salaries were paid up until the new school was built. The exact location of this temporary school is still being investigated. It would appear from the same accounts that the schoolmistress only worked part time as her remuneration for the year June 1872 to June 1873 was £6-7-0d and the church organist £15-0-0d, and again from 1874 to 1875 the schoolmistress' salary for the year was £7-7-2d compared to the organist who received £15-0-0d. Another possibility is that she was a lady of quality and the salary was pocket money.

A School Board was established in Luton in February 1874 after a long period of ignominious wrangling between the Anglican and Nonconformist bodies. The Revd E R Adams, Vicar of Holy Trinity, Biscot, was a member of the board and, very unusual for the time, he was a Liberal. In Luton, Anglican vicars were, in the main, Conservatives and Nonconformist ministers, Liberal. The elected School Board consisted of four Anglicans (known as the prayer book five), one of the five failing to be elected. There were four Nonconformists (known as the Bible five) plus the Vicar of Biscot who voted with the Bible five. The Revd E R Adams wanted a school built at Biscot and another at Leagrave but he had been told by the Anglican authorities that the children should attend a school in Luton. This was unacceptable to Adams who made an agreement with the Liberal members of the School Board that he would support them if they would agree to schools being built in Biscot and Leagrave. This saved

Rear of Biscot (Limbury) School (JGD)

Photographs of Biscot School and Headmaster's House taken just prior to demolition in the 1960s. They were built next to Holy Trinity Churchyard as a Board School in 1876. Although the site is now an Afro-Caribbean Day Centre, the old school can still be seen. (ME)

the children a long walk mornings and evenings. The additional schools at Biscot and Leagrave put an increase on the rates and made poor Adams the most unpopular member of the board.

As today, the School Boards were very concerned about pupil attendance. In view of the compulsory attendance system new laws were put into force. Threats and inducements were used to improve attendance and in many schools medals were presented in bronze, white metal and, in some cases, silver to boost numbers. From C J Peaple's book "The Blockers' Seaside", we learn that medals were presented at Leagrave School and, it is probable, at Limbury-cum-Biscot as well, although I can find no documentary proof.

Letters to The Luton Reporter – January 1875

16th January 1875 – The Old Biscot School

Sir

In your last issue you published a letter from Mr J S Crawley in which he explained his reason for pulling down and removing the school at Biscot. The reason for doing so I imagine will have astonished your readers as much as it did me. He says he pulled down the School House as the windows were broken and he could not get them repaired. I am aware that some mischievous person broke some panes of glass and I am also aware that I paid for the mending of the windows more than once. I do not know if any of the windows were broken when the School House was pulled down. No person can suppose that a man would say he had pulled down a house and carted away all materials because someone had broken the windows.

Before the passing of the Education Act of 1870 Mr Crawley wrote to me stating that in the event of the Act passing, he should require possession of the School. On 10th July 1871 he wrote as follows "I enclose a cheque for my subscription to Biscot School for the past six months, and request you to give me possession as soon as possible. In accordance with his demand I gave up possession of Biscot School, which Mr Crawley forthwith pulled down and used the materials on his estate. I heard at the time that he intended to turn the School into a Blacksmiths Forge but the project did not meet with favour, ere the work of destruction was accomplished.

Mr T Taylor, Mr Crawley's steward, came to the school and carefully removed a few things that were left including a pail and some brushes. I questioned the right of Mr Crawley to pull down the School, but could not afford to go to law. I hired the best cottage in Biscot I could to carry on the school's work, this I have done ever since. I may mention that the School House was so damp that it was hardly fit for habitation.

I suggest that Mr Crawley should not give such humorous reasons for pulling down buildings because of broken windows.

I am Sir Yours Faithfully

E R Adams – Vicar of Biscot

23rd January 1875 – Old Biscot School

Sir

Regarding Mr Adams letter of the 16th January 1875, I affirm that Mr Taylor either spoke or wrote more than once on the subject of broken windows to Mr Adams and the reply he received was that the police had been communicated with but the windows were not mended.

I may have intimated my intention at some time to take back possession of the School but I repeat I was prompted solely by the state of the building. If Mr Adams had a desire for the pail and brushes, he might at the same time have taken the desks etc. The accompanying note will give Mr Adams that information and enable your readers to judge if the want of veracity is justly charged to me.

I am Sir Yours Obediently

J S Crawley

To Mr J S Crawley – 17th January 1875

Sir

At your request I spoke to Mr Adams with regard to the broken windows at the School House at Biscot, and in consequence of their not being repaired after repeated applications, you had the School pulled down.

Mr Adams made application for the desks and forms and had them taken to a cottage in the village.

I remain Yours Respectfully

Thos Taylor

The Education Department, on the report of its inspector, had decided that Biscot and Leagrave needed schools of their own, although Rev James O'Neill, Vicar of Luton, still saw no reason why the children should not walk into Luton to school, as indeed did children from Caddington, Slip End and Woodside until schools were provided there. Plots of land were obtained and plans drawn up for the schools which needless to say were watched over by the Vicar of Biscot as a member of the School Board. The cost of the schools for which money was borrowed from the Public Works Loan Commissioners, worked out at £30-0s-0d per pupil compared with £3-10-0d for the Christ Church Schools built by voluntary effort. Poor Adams, for obvious reasons, was the most unpopular member of the board. Shortly afterwards he relinquished his living and moved to Bedford, but he continued to sit on the board until 1877.

The third school at Biscot was built in 1876 adjacent to Biscot Churchyard, and it was an attractive building with fine decorative brickwork. In style the school was typical mid-nineteenth century Gothic Revival; this was to give the impression that the building reflected the Renaissance quest for learning, with the hope that this may influence the pupils. This Board School at Biscot had in 1902 accommodation for 153 scholars and at this time the Headmistress was Mrs Maidment, who was assisted by Misses Cowley, Ward, Glenister and Craig. The caretaker was Mrs M Bass and the overseers Messrs A Blundell and J Smith. The school, in common with others, gave children an elementary education from five to twelve years.

From 1877 Biscot Church rented both Biscot and Leagrave Schools as Sunday Schools which was a welcomed income for the School Board.

After the Balfour Educational Act of 1902, Biscot School came under the authority of Bedfordshire County Council which was responsible for education in the hamlets surrounding Luton. By 1939 the school at Biscot had 209 scholars and was now under the control of the Local Education Authority, which was responsible for elementary education within Luton Borough and the surrounding hamlets. A school had opened in Norton Road in 1913 for Juniors and Infants which had relieved the overcrowding pressures at the Biscot School. In 1946 however numbers at Biscot had increased to 259, which was to be the high water mark to the relief of the then headmistress Miss Horsley.

During the Second World War the Parish Institute, which once stood in the now church car park, was used by the London County Council for evacuee school children. Also a part of the vicarage stables was converted into a school canteen. Biscot School played its part in making the London children welcome in the village, in the school and in their homes.

Biscot School closed in 1962, with the children transferring to Norton Road. The school building then became a Youth Centre before finally being demolished in the 1990s to make way for a Caribbean Community Centre. Biscot can celebrate with pride over 100 years of education within the village.

Notes of the conversations between Mr Roland Scanes and Mrs Mary Ward, aged ninety-five years, on 19th and 21st July 2003 regarding Biscot School. Mrs Ward recalls the following memories:

"In the late 1950s, pending the completion of the Meads Infants School at Limbury Mead, Luton, I was given the headship of the Infants School adjacent to Holy Trinity Church Biscot. The school and school house were mid Victorian, with two 1939–1945 wartime huts in the school yard, positioned against the wall which overlooked the churchyard.

"At this time due to extensive local housing, the school premises were unable to cope with the extra influx of children. As a result of this, two upstairs rooms in the school house, and the church hall were used as extra class rooms. The schoolhouse rooms each accommodated twelve children. We divided the church hall with flimsy partitions and each section held up to fifty two infants. Because of the overcrowding, as frequently happened, if a child fell against one of those partitions, the partition would fall into the next class. The pictures we had attached to the partition would all fall off, causing chaos.

"All toilets at the school for both pupils and staff were primitive affairs situated as they were outside across the school yard.

"On one occasion when the Vicar had disposed of an old piano in the churchyard, the children recovered some of the hammers with which to play. Some of the children used them to scrape out the mortar of the wall dividing the school house garden from the yard, as a result of which I was greeted one morning by a very glum caretaker with the news that the wall had fallen down.

"When there was a funeral at Biscot Church the Vicar would send word to ask us to arrange our break times so that there was no clash. I remember one occasion when, due to some unforeseen delays, the children leaving the first dinner sitting and those going to the second sitting met the coffin head on. Fortunately they noticed only the beautiful flowers so none were upset.

"Because of the school's age and location many assume it to be a Church School but it belonged to Luton Corporation; however it did lack modern amenities, including electricity, whilst the kitchen of the schoolhouse sported an old fashioned copper wash boiler with space for a coal fire beneath. Like the school the schoolhouse was lit by gas. I well remember an early visit from the Director of Education, Dr Corbett, who was shocked to find gas lighting and no electricity on the premises. The school was heated by a coke boiler which one of my teachers undertook to refuel at lunch times in return for a free school dinner.

"I remember giving a class a lesson about the values of our coinage, using cardboard money, which some of the boys took home to put in the sweet machine at the nearby corner shop. They even had the cheek to tell the shopkeeper his machine was out of order when the cardboard coins failed to work, and to ask for their money back."

Notes taken during conversation between Mrs Mary Sanderson and the author on 21st July 2003 regarding Biscot School in 1962 (its final year):

"At this time the school catered only for mixed infants between the ages of five and seven years. There were a large number of children, and to accommodate them, one large class was held in the school hall, plus the three comparatively modern classrooms built in the playground. The church hall was also used which, being fitted with two wooden sliding partitions, made three additional class rooms. The noises from the adjacent classes made teaching difficult. Classes walking to and from the church hall were also a problem in inclement weather.

"The school was heated by a coke boiler maintained by the staff on a rota system, the teacher on boiler duty being given a free school lunch.

"The toilets were located outside against a playground wall. The toilet at the end of the block was reserved for the staff and, when occupied, the children thought it fun to call your name under the door.

"The front room of the school house was used as the Head Teacher's office, with the staff room upstairs. When the Director of Education visited the school he was shocked to find gas lighting in the staff room. When he asked why there was gas lighting upstairs he was told it was because there was gas lighting downstairs.

"At one time the children en bloc decided they did not like custard for school dinners. The head teacher then told the parents that custard will not be served for school dinners, but would be replaced by yellow blancmange."

CHAPTER 12

Extracts from Biscot/Limbury School Log Book

Headmistress Mrs Jane Maidment

6th October 1899	Start of a new school year, children put into new standards. Miss Lowther came on supply in the Infants room. Parents are upset that the Labour Leaving Certificate Standard has been raised to VI.
13th October 1899	Visited by School Board Officer, Mr Sell, who said that the Labour Leaving Certificate examination was to be held on the 21st October and that this was to be based on Standard V. Nine children will sit the examination.

Report by the Inspector of Schools.
On the whole the school is well taught, especially the first class. There is unsatisfactory teaching in the second and third classes in reading. Order and general tone good, singing and drill deserve praise, the infants' class show little knowledge of numbers.

9th February 1900	Morning by morning the temperature in the classrooms is at freezing point, only reaching a maximum of 40°F with both stoves alight. Heavy falls of snow.
25th May 1900	Surprise visit by School Inspector, complained of untidy state of school. Informed caretaker.
3rd September 1900	Many older scholars absent, the boys are working in the fields and the girls gleaning.
5th October 1900	Children were placed into their new classes, though those in Standard I will occasionally go into the Infants' room to keep up their singing and drill exercises until the visit of H M Inspector on 15th inst.
22nd February 1901	H M Inspector visited the school and spoke of urgent need of a fire guard in the main room and complained of the ventilation. Lost my best scholar and nicest boy – gone to work.
12th July 1901	School closed on Wednesday because of Primitive Methodist Sunday School treat. Cookery was therefore taken on Thursday morning.
1st July 1904	Children had half day holiday because of Band of Hope treat.
24th February 1905	Gardening lessons in class and school garden.
27th March 1905	Nine children received badges for perfect attendance in the last quarter.
6th October 1905	The oil lamps have gone to Caddington school now that gas is put in here.
24th November 1905	Two boys punished for swearing and fighting in the playground.
1st December 1905	Mr Cutler came about Bygrave and Smith throwing stones at his pigeons and breaking tiles

A policeman called later to see these boys and said that the former was always being complained of, especially about insulting and annoying old people.

22nd December 1905   Broke up for Christmas, the children had tea in school and each took home a bag which contained an orange, an apple and a mince pie.

27th February 1906   Visit by H M Inspector – ventilation and heating far from satisfactory. The desks on the gallery are far too low for all but the very smallest of infants.

25th January 1907   Attendance has fallen off through severe weather. Thermometer at 32°F in the morning inspite of two fires, it was 42°F when we left in the afternoon.

19th July 1907   Visit on Thursday morning by Mr Blundell of Limbury Manor with his sister in law from New Zealand. She spoke to the children about that country and said that she would come and speak to them again.

13th September 1907   School opened on the 9th after the holiday but closed again for the rest of the week by the manager's direction because of the harvest.

6th December 1907   Visit by H M Inspector noted a temperature of 50°F at 11.30am. The thermometer has been read three times a day for a fortnight, highest temperature reached 58°F.

17th January 1908   Visit by H M Inspector who remarked on the school room gallery still being there.

31st January 1908   A new boiler was put in on Saturday, it was quite warm in the class room at 9.00am, it was 57°F and 60°F at 12 o'clock.

1st March 1912	Several children away with ring worm, I have reported a very dirty family to the S P C C.
19th April 1912	Glad it is warmer so that the overcrowded Infants room can be relieved by holding classes in the playground. Much interest shown in the eclipse of the Sun.
10th May 1912	Heat making children restless. Babies class taken out of doors.
24th May 1912	Empire Day – The Vicar hoisted the flag in the playground, children marched past, saluted and sang the National Anthem.
15th November 1912	Jane Maidment retired as Headmistress after 25 years 8 months service at the school.
15th September 1913	This morning I L Mariner commenced duties as Headmistress of Limbury C School. The school opens today as a new Infants School which includes Standard I. Other children transferred to Norton Road School.
13th March 1914	Attendance has been dreadful, 62.9%, this has been due to Bronchitis, Flu' and severe colds.
20th March 1914	School closed due to heavy falls of snow
1st May 1914	27 cases of Mumps and 5 of Measles
4th May 1914	School closed until 25th May due to Mumps
3rd July 1914	Very hot week, violent thunderstorms on Wednesday, many scholars absent. There is still much sickness and attendance is low.
24th July 1914	School closed all day Wednesday for Biscot Church Sunday School treat.
25th September 1914	School opened after 7 weeks closure. Extension of two weeks necessary as, in consequence of the war, soldiers have been billeted in the school room.

21st December 1914	Fearful weather, only 46 scholars present from 128 on books.
8th January 1915	Attendance very bad only 64%, many scholars are ill and the weather has been fearful.
12th February 1915	Weather very bad. School closed all week.
19th March 1915	Coldest day this winter, half the children absent; unable to keep to time table. The children were kept moving frequently to keep warm.
7th May 1915	Have promoted 8 scholars from the Baby room to Class III this week.
25th June 1915	Our classes have been weakened lately by the constant entry of backward scholars.
15th November 1915	Cicely E Kingham commenced duties as Headmistress.
25th February 1916 to end of March 1916	Very poor attendance due to fearful weather, rain and snow. With the consent of the Rev S Collins the school was closed for the most of this period.
19th May 1916	Owing to gradual addition to the Babies class, 5 children were promoted from Class I to Standard I, 10 from Class II to Class I and 7 from Babies to Class II. I have admitted 6 children this week all over 5 years of age.
16th January 1920	Dr Hardman inspected 32 children admitted to the school over the past year, nearly all mothers being present. Mr Cooper the school dentist inspected 82 children's teeth, this occupied most of the morning.
5th April 1921	Mrs L M Horne commenced her duties as Headmistress.
15th June 1926	Whole day's holiday for Church Sunday School treat to Bricket Wood.

28th March 1927	School dentist Mr Cooper visited the school to treat the children, this took all day. Teeth were extracted at the Baptist Chapel school room.
22nd November 1928	The name of this school in future will be The Luton, Limbury Infants Council School No 17.
26th November 1930	As an extra classroom we are using the Chapel Sunday School room. There are no pegs for hanging clothes, they are laid on forms, therefore no chance to dry in wet weather. It was extremely cold on Thursday the radiators barely warm. The thermometer registered 52°F when placed over the radiator. It was not warm enough for the children to sit with their outdoor clothes off.
4th April 1932	113 children aged 7 years and over were transferred to Norton Road School. This school is now purely an Infants department.
5th May 1941	The number of children on the school books has now reached 250, part of the increase was due to the influx of children from the bombed areas of London following heavy air raids.
16th March 1942	Number of children on books has now reached 280; Director of Education Mr Cutter came to see if the Church Institute could be used to ease overcrowding. Air Raid Wardens came to the school to check children's gas masks.
14th June 1942	Approx 80 children now have school dinners, the dinner bus leaves at 12.10 and frequently does not return until 1.20. As afternoon school commences at 1.30 this leaves little or no break for the teachers. A rota has to be devised to give the teachers a little breathing space before afternoon school.

23rd May 1944	Mr Webb the Dental Surgeon examined the teeth of all the 172 children present. The examination took place at the end of the main room.
24th May 1944	Empire Day lessons taken in the upper classes on Empire topics. In the afternoon the whole school marched around the premises carrying flags.
16th June 1944	Vauxhall Motors are having holidays from today. A number of children are affected.
30th June 1944	The Air Raid warning siren went off about 8.58 am; children went into the shelters.
10th July 1944	Today I admitted 10 more evacuees from various parts of London
14th August 1944	Re-opened after summer holidays, admitted only 30 local 5-year-old children and 17 evacuees.
6th November 1944	We started work in the Church Parish Room with Class III.
25th January 1945	A hard frost and snow all week. No water to flush the lavatories, all water had to be carried from the school house.
29th January 1945	School closed due to frozen lavatories.
3rd March 1945	Cases of measles increasing, attendance 73.4%, 291 children on books.
8th & 9th May 1945	V E Day holidays.
10th May 1945	Vauxhall workers still on holiday, only 84 children in school.
11th May 1945	Evacuees gradually drifting back to London.
4th October 1945	A medical inspection was to be held in the Parish Institute today, a cold and foggy morning. The doctor refused to examine infants without a heated room. We transferred the children to a classroom with a fire.

28th February 1946   Miss Hughes called this afternoon about the possibility of a hot water supply for the main school. At present there is only a pail over the stove and a kettle over a gas ring.

22nd May 1953   School closed today for Whitsun and Coronation holidays. The children were given entertainment and tea. All went home with a Coronation Mug.

12th June 1953   53 children were taken to the Odeon Cinema to see "A Queen is Crowned".

7th April 1954   This term despite a great deal of sickness among the children, has been a happy one.

22nd January 1958   It has been snowing for two days. Extra time is allowed for changing wellingtons and drying wet clothes.

4th December 1958   20 children were immunised against diphtheria.

8th January 1959   Snow is falling. One third of school away with measles.

23rd March 1960   At a managers' meeting concern was expressed regarding the overcrowding conditions. A new school to serve the area will be built ASAP on the Limbury Mead Estate.

20th July 1962   Today Limbury Infants School finishes as an independent unit. On 4th September it will open as the Infants Department of Norton Road Junior Mixed. I leave today, as do most of the staff. I have enjoyed the inconveniences of Limbury School – *Mary Ward, Headmistress*.

CHAPTER 13

The Consecration of

Holy Trinity Church, Biscot

Taken from The Luton Reporter, 6th June 1868

hrough the munificence of John Sambrooke Crawley Esq, of Stockwood Park, a neat little church has been erected for the use of the inhabitants of the new district of Biscott. On Tuesday last, 2nd June 1868 this church which is only just finished, having been rather a long time in hand, was consecrated by the Right Rev the Lord Bishop of Ely.

The consecration service was announced for eleven o'clock, and a little before this hour several carriages were seen approaching Biscott from Luton, and probably some fifty or sixty persons went on foot, so that the greater part of the congregation which crowded the church consisted of Lutonians.

The stained and varnished pews, which afford accommodation for about 200 are comfortably contrived, and will, we should say, except on days few and far between, be enough for all the wants of the population of this village.

At the entrance to the chancel which is tastefully fitted up, there is a screen of carved work, to the right of which stands the pulpit, which is

John Sambrooke Crawley – Founder and Patron of Holy Trinity Church, Biscot (DK)

Early view of Biscot Church and School taken from the field beyond the then Churchyard boundary wall (KC)

of white stone tastefully carved, and but for its size might be taken at a glance for an immense font. A brass stand is provided for the use of the officiating clergy-man, but his lordship laid his sermon book on the stone, only using the brass stand once or twice as a rest for his arm.

The font is of white stone carved after an allegorical design, which is very pretty and is suggestive of devoutness and humility. The wall of the chancel over the communion table, which was covered with a beautiful cloth bearing the sign of the cross, was decorated by encaustic tiles with a pretty effect.

The roof is of plain deal stained, but it is very strong, capable of enduring for several generations. The church is built of white brick with bath-stone dressings which look very well outside, but inside the bare walls look rather cold, although the work is good.

The church stands in the centre of three acres of ground, which has been levelled and fenced in and which after the ceremonial within the building was solemnly dedicated for ever for the use of the inhabitants of Biscott as a burial place for their dead.

The bishop was attended by his chaplain and secretary, and by the Right Rev the Lord Bishop of Sierra Leone, the Rev F Hose, Rev J Lee, Rev Mr Green, Rev Mr Prescott, Rev M. Iggulden, Rev H B Smyth, Rev Mr Adams, the rector of the newly consecrated church, and other clergymen. The Rev J O'Neill and the Rev H Tite were also present. Amongst the congregation were Mr J S Crawley, Mr Kershaw and family, Mr J G Shepherd and family, Mr Seymour, Mr Wright and lady, of St Johns College, Mr James Higgins, Mr George Bailey, Mr and Mrs Cook, Mr Kidman and family, Mr Scarborough, Mr Taylor, Rev R Stevenson, Rev J D Stevens, &c., &c.

On entering the church, his lordship's secretary read a document setting forth that by a deed dated 17th June 1857, John Sambrooke Crawley Esq, conveyed to the Ecclesiastical Commissioners for England for the spiritual use of the inhabitants of Biscott a piece of land containing a little over three acres, and that the new church had been erected on a portion of the said land, and was finished and ready for consecration, and that the remaining portion of the said land, which was intended as a burial ground, had been properly prepared, levelled, and enclosed, and was likewise in a state fit for consecration. That the said church had been endowed by the said John Sambrooke Crawley Esq, with tithes amounting to the sum of £148 14s 5d per annum, to which the said Ecclesiastical Commissioners have added the sum of £50. That on the 20th day of November 1866, by an Order in Council, a district for spiritual purposes was assigned to the church, and therefore his lordship by his authority according to law did consecrate the same to Almighty God for the purpose of divine worship therein according to the rites and ceremonies of the United Church of England and Ireland, as by law established, for the use of the inhabitants of the said district for ever.

Then followed the service, during which Mr Cokayne, organist of

Christ Church, presided at the harmonium assisted by one or two of the choristers of Christ Church. Before the sermon, the choir sang the 244th hymn: "Christ is made the sure Foundation,

     Christ the head and corner stone."

For his text his Lordship selected the sixteenth verse of the chapter of St Paul's Epistle to the Corinthians – "Know ye not that ye are the temple of God, and that the spirit of God dwelleth in you?" and dwelt for half-an-hour on the office assigned of the Holy Spirit in the work of human redemption.

A collection was made towards building a house for the rector.

After the benediction, his lordship and the clergy-men in attendance walked over the burial ground, and then it was formally set apart to its future use, the bishop's chaplain reading the sentence of consecration.

CHAPTER 14

Tour of Biscot Church

*B*iscot Church was built in 1868 through the munificence of Mr John Sambrooke Crawley, Lord of the Manor of Biscot, who provided both the land and the money. He also provided for a large vicarage which once stood beside it.

The church is surrounded by a large churchyard of over three acres and includes some fine trees, which give it a rural atmosphere, signifying

Rear of Holy Trinity Church (CC)

Front of Holy Trinity Church and Churchyard (CC)

Biscot's past village status. The building is typical mid-Victorian design, with its Gothic Revival shapes and arches so popular at the time for municipal buildings, schools and churches.

The large churchyard at Biscot gives the church its rural setting, the total area being close on four acres. Its fauna and flora have been mentioned in the histories of Bedfordshire, although habitat for wild life has to be weighed against the upkeep and maintenance of the churchyard. We may not have the very famous buried at Biscot, although each grave will yield a story for you to uncover. There are approximately 4,000 souls laying here and although the churchyard is virtually closed there are a few family spaces. In the past the churchyard served other churches in the area besides Anglican and the trust set up to administer the churchyard is represented from them.

In Biscot Churchyard there are a number of war graves, which are maintained on behalf of The War Graves Commissioners which can be a rich source of study and sadness. From one headstone we learn that his name was John (Jack) Stanley Fensome aged twenty years buried 8th January 1941.

Jack whose home was in Bishopscote Road was a Sergeant in the RAF and with five others was on a training flight in a Wellington bomber in Scotland over Loch Ness. During the flight the plane got into difficulties, and the six trainees were ordered to parachute out. All landed safely except for Jack whose parachute failed to open. The two man air crew managed to ditch the plane in Loch Ness and using a rubber dingy paddle to the shore. The plane was found in 1980 and was restored at Brooklands.

The church consists of a nave and chancel, a porch on the northern side of the nave, and a small transept on the north side of the chancel. On the south side of the chancel is an organ chamber and a small vestry. The length of the church is approximately 100 feet, including the chancel which is 36 feet. The width of the chancel is approximately 26 feet and the nave approximately 40 feet. The pews are stained and varnished and can comfortably accommodate over 200 souls.

The glass doors on the porch at the main entrance to the Church were donated by Mrs Elsie Willison in memory of her parents and her husband.

Entering the Church from the porch, on the right can be seen the tall two-light West Window with mullions and stone dressings, its stained glass signifying Alpha and Omega, the beginning and the end. Dedicated on the Sunday after Christmas, 29th December 1918. The left light depicts Jesus with children "Suffer the little children to come unto Me" and the right light, The Ascension "He ascended into Heaven".

Moving up the nave, which is paved with red and black tiles, and taking care not to walk on the heating gratings with high-heeled shoes, we pass two Mothers Union banners. On the north side of the nave are two plain

Memorial to John Sambrooke Crawley's second wife (CC)

windows, one three lights and the other two lights. We now approach the chancel steps where a hand rail is provided and before renovation was carried out in the late 1950s here stood a carved oak screen. Here also is our Book of Remembrance dedicated to Winifred Shewring and Blanche Hook.

The arch which opens into the north transept from the choir stalls in the chancel is supported by a massive pillar – the base and cap is of Bath stone and the column of polished Aberdeen granite. On the left past the transept is a memorial to Mr John Sambrooke Crawley's second wife Maria who died 16th September 1875 aged eighty-two. There is also a processional cross on an oak staff used on high days. This is a memorial to Mr A Lathwell who in 1939 had served as Vicar's Warden for twenty years.

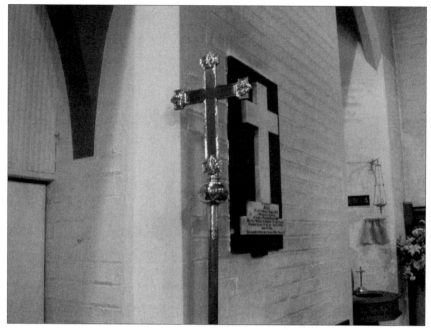

Processional Cross with the Aumbry in the background (CC)

We are not able to enter the sanctuary, but from the altar rail can be seen a two-light stained glass window on the north wall depicting "The Blessed Virgin Mary and Child" in one light and "The Good Shepherd" in the other; this window was given by Elizabeth Durham Smith and dedicated on Trinity Sunday, 15th June 1919 by the Rt Revd Bishop E N Hodges.

On the east wall to the left of the altar is the aumbry where the emergency sacrament is kept. Above this is the aumbry light dedicated in memory of Meg and Reg Barker. This is kept alight when the sacrament is present. Above the altar is the East Window with three-light stained glass with mullions and stone dressings depicting on the left, "St Mary & Angel", dedicated to the Glory of God, Trinity Sunday, 26th May 1918 by grateful Parishioners and friends, in the centre, "Christ Crucified &

The Altar (CC)

Mary Magdalene", to the Glory of God and in loving memory of Julia Redding erected by her Husband on his birthday, 26th May 1918, and on the right "St John & Angel", in commemoration of the Jubilee of the consecration of this Church. This window was dedicated by the Rt Revd Bishop E N Hodges, Archdeacon of Bedford.

The altar frontal is changed with the Church's seasonal colours, with green being the colour for Trinity.

On the small table to the right of the altar is the water for ritual ablutions and the vessels for water and wine. Below the window on the south wall is a stone basin let into the wall which is used to contain holy water. Also on the wall near to us is a brass plaque listing the incumbents from the first vicar of Holy Trinity.

On our right is a door leading to the vestry, in which is housed an ancient iron chest. Holy Trinity has a tangible connection with the Moat House, for this iron chest is one of two found buried on Moat (House) Farm some time shortly after 1850. The land belonging as it did to Squire Crawley, the chests passed into his possession, he gave one chest to Holy Trinity, Biscot and the other was placed in his house at Stockwood. The front of the chests, whose lids are fitted with a combination of locks, are ornamented with an armorial which appears, according to Austin, to be the Eagles and Crown of Austria. The chests, which probably date from the early part of the seventeenth century, were perhaps intended as deed boxes, but are of particularly robust construction – a function similar to that of a modern safe.

Above the door is a brass plaque in memory of John Sambrooke Crawley who provided the church for the people of Biscot. He was born on 29th April 1823, and died on 22nd September 1895. The plaque to the right above the choir stalls is in memory of Arthur Charles Worsley who was a chorister in this church for over fifty years, dying at the age of sixty-two on 9th January 1949.

The piped organ was installed in 1915 and dedicated on 29th July by the Rev A Thomas. For this occasion the organist was Mr F Gostelow FRCO and, as recalled by Mrs F Howe, the first Hymn sung was "When Morning Gilds the Skies". The bellows for the organ were activated by a hydraulic engine, replaced in 1938 by an electric motor which was again replaced in 1951.

Gas had been in use for many years since 1906, but the original lighting in the church was by oil lamps, the holes for the lamp holders can be seen in the book rests of the pews. Electricity had been installed in Holy Trinity Church in 1927 as the result of an envelope scheme organised by a special committee convened for the purpose.

Walking back down the chancel steps we can see the decorated stone pulpit, to our left, with a brass stand; on the front of the pulpit is a carved head said to be in the likeness of Squire Crawley.

Ancient Iron Chest (CC)

The Organ (CC)

The Pulpit (decorated for a Flower Festival) (CC)

The first stained glass window we come to on the south side of the nave depicts the Annunciation and was presented by the parents of Arthur Jesse Little, a former choir boy and communicant at Biscot, killed in action in France aged twenty years. A brass plaque below the window informs us that he died on 30th August 1918, so near to the end of the war. The window was dedicated by the Revd F C Mahoney on Trinity Sunday, 30th May 1920.

The second stained glass window we come to on this side of the nave has three lights, and depicts Christ's mental agony in the garden of Gethsemany before His arrest and Crucifixion. It was dedicated on 15th June 1919 by Bishop E N Hodges. The left light depicts "the Disciples sleeping" and was given by Mr John Redding, the centre light depicts "Jesus in the garden" given by the congregation, and the right light, an Angel with "The Cup" as a memorial to Mr F A Cowdrey by the choir.

The Font (CC)

The Lych-gate and War Memorial (CC)

Facing the west end of the church, below its large stained glass window is an impressive white stone font, highly decorated.

The Lych-gate at the entrance to the churchyard is a general memorial to those who died in the Great War and was dedicated on 4th November 1919 by Bishop E N Hodges. The inscription reads:

Biscot Parish Church War Memorial 1914–1919

Erected in Ever Grateful Memory of the Fallen.

"Greater Love Has No Man Than This,

That a Man Lay Down His Life For His Friends".

CHAPTER 15

Life and Times of
Holy Trinity Church, Biscot

*I*n this chapter we look at the every day life at Biscot through the Vestry meetings, yearly accounts and, most important of all, memories. The first incumbent to hold the living at Holy Trinity Church Biscot was Edward Richard Adams, whose induction took place in 1866. Two years later the Church was consecrated by the Rt Rev Bishop E N Hodges.

On 2nd July 1868 the first vestry meeting was held; present were Rev E R Adams in the chair, and Messrs Thomas Kidman and Jonathan Seymour. Mr T Kidman was nominated as Vicar's Warden, and Mr J Seymour was proposed as Parish Warden by Mr T Kidman and seconded by Rev E R Adams.

It was mentioned that certain articles were necessary for the service of the Church, such as grave digging tools, bier, also a cupboard and hat pegs in the vicar's vestry, covers for the church furniture. The churchwardens were requested to provide the same.

It was agreed that persons retaining a pew, should make an offering of one pound per annum towards the service of the Church, and that collections should be made at intervals for the same purpose.

The meeting was then dissolved.   Signed *Edw R Adams Vicar*

The accounts for 1869 showed a credit balance of 4s-4d; this apparently trivial sum must be put in context of the monetary values of the time. A small harmonium was purchased in that year for three pounds, the cost being met out of a donation made by Madam de Falbe of Luton Hoo.

In the 1871 accounts it is recorded that 48 pounds of candles were used in that financial year at a cost of one shilling per pound and that thirteen quarts of paraffin were consumed at a cost of 7s-11d (at this time the Church was lit by oil lamps). Expenditure was also made for washing surplices at 1s-3d, cleaning the Church £3-17s-6d, and sweeping the Church chimney at 2s-0d.

From the 1872 accounts we learn that a new harmonium was purchased at a cost of £20, and that the organist, Mr J L Torey, was paid £5-19s-0d for the year. Again 48 pounds of candles were used and fourteen quarts of paraffin, heating costs were 5s-0d for wood and £4-13s-0d for coal. Three bottles of sacramental wine were consumed. Mr Smith as bell ringer was paid 5s-0d for the year, as per Mr J S Crawley's bequest, and for other Church services £2-4s-0d.

Mrs Bass was paid £3-18s-0d for cleaning the church, and 2s-6d for washing surplices. The total receipts for the year were £69-10s-9d, total expenditure £62-17s-3½d. Pew rents accounted for £16-2s-0d of the income. The churchwardens were now John Kinder and Jonathan Seymour.

In the 1873 accounts we learn that collections were made for; the Luton Cottage Hospital, the poor of the parish, the schoolmistress, and the organist's salary which for that year was £15-0s-0d. The Vicar finally got a cupboard for the vestry at a cost of 13s-0d and the wine had gone up to four bottles. This year Mrs T Bass was assisted by Mrs G Bass in the cleaning of the church and the washing of the surplices, sharing the salary which amounted to £4-4s-0d. Mr James Smith continued ringing the bells and other services in the church and was paid £3-18s-0d. Churchwardens were now Mr J Kinder and Mr E Bates.

The 1874 accounts give an insight into the social conditions of the time, for it lists collections for the clothing club, poor married women, and the poor of the parish. Church expenditure also included the organist's (Mr J L Torley) salary at £15-0-0d for the year, school mistress £10-3s-5½d (part salary), Sunday School excursion £5-14s-2¾d, and the Bengal famine £6-17s-0d, plus general upkeep expenses. The church, as can be seen, took on responsibilities which these days are the domain of the social services.

The Revd E R Adams was succeeded in 1876 by the Revd George Morris who, however, only held the living for a year, to be followed as vicar by Robert Fisher. The Revd Robert Fisher was presented by Mr J S Crawley to the living of Biscot in 1877. Robert Fisher was vexed by some of the spinster ladies of the congregation who never failed to remind him of the occasions on which he had previously preached the same sermons. Robert Fisher who it was said possessed no sense of humour effectually got the better of his lady critics by putting fresh texts to his sermons. The recollection of those sermons preached at Biscot is that they were sound orthodox discourses from the point of view of the Church of England. Robert Fisher's ministry appeared to be one of relatively uneventful consolidation.

From the 1878 accounts the church is being cleaned at a cost of £4-2s-0d per year by Mrs Bass, who also washed the surplices seven times that year for 10s-6d. Mr Torey was paid £20 for playing the organ, and Mr Jackson £2-17s-0d for ringing the bells each week plus three Holy days. The statement of the accounts also records that a very large debt is now owing to the churchwardens of £38-5s-1d, the churchwardens were having to put their hands in their pockets to keep the church solvent. Proposals were offered that subscriptions be made, or increased offertories, or some other way found to reduce the debt. The churchwardens at this time were Mr Jno Kinder and Mr Thos Kidman.

The 1879 accounts showed that church income over expenditure, which included services to the sick and poor was 10s-1d, however nearly £38 was still owed the Churchwardens. The Vicar and Churchwardens made the following plea at the end of the statement:

'The Vicar and Churchwardens of Biscot regret to state that notwithstanding the multiplication of offertories during the past year, combined with the strictest economy on their part, there is still owing the sum of £37-15s-0d, a diminution of only 10s-1d as compared with last year, when there was a balance due to the Churchwardens of £38-5s-1d. Under these circumstances, they venture to bring, not only before the Congregation, but also before the Owners and Occupiers of land in the Parish generally (and the well-wishers of the church at large), the present position of affairs; and respectfully to solicit them to assist, as far as possible; in sustaining the efficiency of the services; as well as in maintaining the Sunday Schools at Biscot and Leagrave; and the other parochial machinery in this scattered Parish; comprising as it does so large a percentage of the operative class. To be compelled to curtail or to give up any of these various means for benefiting the Parish; would they feel, be a matter of regret.

'The Vicar or Churchwardens will most thankfully receive and acknowledge any Subscriptions or Donations in aid of the liquidation of the debt.'

By the time a statement of the accounts was made in 1882 it is clear that economies were being implemented. Turnover had dropped by a half to £42-12s-10d and the amount owing to the Churchwardens now stood at £12-16s-7½d. In the accounts there is no mention of heating or lighting costs nor of payment to the organist. Social payments to the poor and needy have also been reduced. Mr John Jackson rang the bells for £2-18s-0d for the year and his wife is now cleaning the church for £4-8s-0d.

Donations were given to improve the lighting of the church amounting to £16-2s-6d, and lamps and standards were purchased. At the end of the statement an NB advised that additional lighting is still required.

From the 1893 accounts among those giving donations was Mr J W Green of Luton. The organist was now Miss Kidman who was paid £5-0-0d for the year, plus donations amounting to £6-2s-10½d. In this year new lamps for the chancel were supplied. Mr and Mrs Jackson were paid a total of £7-17s-6d for bell ringing, cleaning the church and washing surplices. Outstanding to the Churchwardens was £2-5s-3½d, turnover being £53-1s-5d. The churchwardens were Mr John Cumberland and Mr James Day Browning.

In 1894 the Revd Erskine William Langmore was inducted as Vicar, taking over the living from Robert Fisher who had been Vicar for seventeen years. The Revd Erskine Langmore it has been said was not averse to taking something to keep out the cold before giving the sermon. Although he swayed many times when in the pulpit, only once did he fall out. Towards the end of his incumbency in 1903 a subscription was started for a Mission Church at Leagrave, which was in time to mature as the independent daughter parish of St Luke.

The Vestry meeting held on 25th April 1895 caught the eyes of the local press and the following article appeared in the "Luton News":

Biscot Vestry Meeting 'Wanted – A Warden'. On Friday, the annual vestry meeting was held. The Vicar (Rev E W Langmore) presided. The accounts which last year showed a balance in hand of £3-18s-11d, this year have a deficiency of £3-2s-6d. Mr J H Anstee, Lewsey, declined to act again as Vicar's warden, therefore the Vicar nominated Mr Alfred, stationmaster Leagrave, in his place. Mr Browning, Bramingham was nominated people's warden and Mr Chamberlain, Leagrave Hall, was also named by an amendment, but as both gentlemen positively refused to stand, the meeting had

LIST OF FEES, 1895.

𝔓𝔞𝔯𝔦𝔰𝔥 of 𝔅𝔦𝔰𝔠𝔬𝔱. 𝔇𝔦𝔬𝔠𝔢𝔰𝔢 of 𝔈𝔩𝔶.

MARRIAGE.

	Vicar.	Clerk.	Sexton.	Total.
	£ s. d.	£ s. d.	£ s. d.	£ s. d.
Publishing Banns	0 1 0	0 1 0	... ...	0 2 0
Certificate of Banns	0 1 0	... ...	... ...	0 1 0
Marriage after Banns	0 5 0	0 2 6	... ...	0 7 6
„ by License	0 10 0	0 5 0	... ...	0 15 0
Certificate with stamp	0 2 7	... ...	... ...	0 2 7

BURIAL.

	Vicar.	Clerk.	Sexton.	Total.
	£ s. d.	£ s. d.	£ s. d.	£ s. d.
§Earth Grave, 4ft. 6in. deep *	0 3 0	0 1 0	0 2 0	0 6 0
Single Brick Grave	1 0 0	0 5 0	0 5 0	1 10 0
*Double „	1 10 0	0 7 6	0 7 6	2 5 0
Re-opening above	0 10 0	0 2 6	0 2 6	0 15 0
Vault for 2 persons	2 0 0	0 10 0	0 10 0	3 0 0
„ 4 „	6 0 0	1 0 0	1 0 0	8 0 0
„ Each extra	2 0 0	1 0 0	1 0 0	4 0 0
Re-opening Vault	1 0 0	0 5 0	0 5 0	1 10 0
Earth Grave for Child under 12 years ...	0 2 0	0 1 6	0 2 0	0 5 6
Still-born Infant	0 1 6	0 1 0	0 2 0	0 4 6
Stamped Certificate of Burial	0 2 7	... ...	... ...	0 2 7

§ Each extra foot in depth, 2/-.   *For more than two at same rate.

N.B.—The digging, bricking, &c., is contracted for by the friends of the deceased.

TOLLING BELL.

The charge for the "Passing Bell" for a quarter-of-an hour is Sixpence, to be paid to the Clerk.

Bell at Funeral, Sixpence; to be paid to the Clerk.

For turfing or banking up a Grave, after the first time, the Sexton is entitled to a fee of a shilling, or more, according to the work done.

Cast-iron Grave Marks, numbered, may be had for 1/6; also cast-iron Memorials from 5/-, on application to the Vicar.

MONUMENTS.

	Vicar.	Clerk.	Sexton.	Total.
	£ s. d.	£ s. d.	£ s. d.	£ s. d.
Plain Head and Foot Stone or Cross, 4ft. high ...	0 10 6	0 2 6	... ...	0 13 0
For every foot or portion of foot extra	0 2 6	0 0 6	... ...	0 3 0
Grave Enclosure, stone or metal, 1ft. high ...	0 5 0	0 1 0	... ...	0 6 0
Every extra foot or portion of foot	0 2 6	0 0 6	... ...	0 3 0
Tablet in Church, 1 square foot or portion of foot	1 0 0	0 5 0	... ...	1 5 0
Cast-Iron or Wood Memorials, if over 1ft. high ...	0 1 6	... ...	0 1 0	0 2 6
„ „ „ „ 2ft. „ ...	0 2 6	... ...	0 1 6	0 4 0
„ „ „ „ 3ft. „ ...	0 4 0	... ...	0 2 6	0 6 6
[One foot and under free.]				

The Plan of any Head or Foot Stone, together with any Inscription in the Churchyard or Church, must be submitted to and approved by the Incumbent.

List of Fees 1895 (Holy Trinity Church records)

to look about for someone else, the Vicar suggesting it should be a churchman. Mr Browning said, "Not necessarily, it doesn't matter whether he is church or chapel if he is a ratepayer." Ultimately, after several names had been suggested with no better result, Mr Craig, Moat Farm, was (although absent) put in for the people. Should he also decline to act, the place will go a-begging. Mr Walker proposed a vote of thanks to the retiring churchwardens, which was carried unanimously.

Vestry Meeting – 11th April 1902

At the annual vestry meeting held on Friday morning last, the Vicar reported that the trustees of Richard's Charity had finally decided to adhere to their resolution of the previous year, to limit the benefits of the Charity to the inhabitants of the town of Luton. Accordingly Biscot parish would receive no more for the sick and poor from this source. The subject of the Mission Church at Leagrave was discussed, and it was determined to start a subscription list for the purpose. The Bishop and Archdeacon had promised to help.

A letter was read from the Secretary of the Diocesan Trust, accepting the conveyance of land at Leagrave from Mr J Cumberland, and appointing local administrative trustees according to the rules of the Trust. It was resolved to have a map of the parish prepared. Messrs G E Aldred and F Deuxberry were re-appointed Churchwardens, and they nominated Messrs D Stangham and Jos Johnson as their sidesmen. The Vicar pointed out that this year, for the first time, the sidesmen as well as the churchwardens were cited to attend the Archdeacon's visitation at Dunstable on Wednesday, 9th April. At the close of the Vestry meeting the church accounts were read out and showed a balance in hand, both on the general and special accounts: in the former case the surplus being £1-17s-4d and in the latter £1-1s- 0d.

The fencing of the Leagrave Church ground, it was reported, had also

Vicar of Holy Trinity Church with the Choir in the early 1900s (JR)

been paid for. With regard to the Nurse Fund, the Vicar had sent eighteen shillings as a gratuity to Nurse Sarll in appreciation of her visits to the poor and sick of the parish.

From The Luton and District Year Book for 1902, Biscot with Limbury is described as a village about two miles from Luton and one mile from Leagrave Station with a population of 400. The Board School is under the control of the Luton School Board, and has accommodation for 153 scholars. The head-mistress is Mrs Maidment, who is assisted by Misses Cowley, Ward, Glenister and Craig. The caretaker is Mrs M A Bass. The overseers of the school are Messrs A Blundell and James Smith; the assistant overseer and Parish Council Clerk is Mr G Maidment. During the winter a carpentry class is held under the auspices of the Beds County Council, Mr Maidment being the teacher. There is a flourishing Band of Hope with about 130 members; the meetings are held in the school

Manoeuvres at the back of the Holy Trinity Churchyard in the First World War (LR)

and are conducted on non-sectarian lines, the President being also Mr Maidment. (It is clear that Mr and Mrs Maidment are well known figures in the life of Biscot). There are two postal collections, and two deliveries of letters each day, Sundays excepted.

In 1903 when Alfred Steele Fairbrother became Vicar of Holy Trinity, Biscot, the boundary of the Ecclesiastical Parishes of Christ Church and Biscot was adjusted.

The balance sheet for the year ending Easter 1906 showed that the Luton Gas Co provided fittings and gas for the church for a cost of £16-4s-3d. A piano for the Sunday School was hired for ten shillings, but later one was purchased at a cost of twenty shillings. Fire insurance cost £2-5s-0d and Sunday School Treats etc amounted to £4-19s-6d. Gifts were made to the poor amounting to £10-18s-8d which included sacks of coal and a bath chair. The churchwardens were Evan William Lee and Frederick Deuxberry.

Biscot Camp 1916 (PW)

A garden party was held on 29th June 1907 at 1 Neville Road, with a dance in the evening at the Neville Hall; a whist drive was held a week before. The profit from these social events totalled £91-19-2d (no mean figure for the time).

In 1913 the Revd A S Fairbrother was succeeded by Sidney Herbert Collins who was remembered with affection for his dignified and sincere personality. He was Vicar of Holy Trinity for seventeen years to 1930, thus spanning the period of the First World War and its difficult aftermath.

In 1914 Mr F Crawley made a gift of one acre and one rood adjoining the then churchyard for its future extension, the church paying the extension consecration fee of £3- 8s-0d.

During the 1914–1918 war a large military camp was set up near the Biscot Mill, and it was mainly a tented camp with some wooden huts. Luton was host to thousands of servicemen who were quartered in and on the outskirts of the town. On 10th April 1916 Princess Victoria Louise, eldest daughter of Queen Victoria, visited Biscot Camp to open a new

Biscot Camp 1916 (PW)

Gunners at Biscot Camp in 1916 posing with a local wide boy and his make-shift stall (KC)

These Luton boys are members of the King's Royal Corps cadets at Biscot Camp in 1914. (KC)

Biscot Camp Christmas 1917 (PW)

YMCA hut named after her. In 1918 there was snow on the ground into late April which made living under canvas very difficult, but they probably preferred Biscot mud to that of Flanders.

From the Biscot Parish Church balance sheet for the year ending 24th April 1916, we learn that collections were made for the Lych-gate, Organ Fund, Church Army War Fund, Sailors and Soldiers Workshop Fund (Lord Roberts Memorial), and the Sunday Schools. Expenditure included radiators for St Luke's, Leagrave, and insurance was taken out against air raid risks from German airships at a cost of £5-5s-0d. The organist's salary for the year stood at £10-0-0d. Churchwardens for that year were Mr William Powe and Mr S W Hull.

1918 was the Jubilee of the consecration of Holy Trinity Church, coinciding with the end of the Great War. This resulted in the raising of a number of memorials in the church, being mainly in the form of stained glass windows. The Lych-gate is a general memorial to those who fell in the Great War. Full details are to be found in the chapter relating to the tour of the church.

The year 1923 witnessed the dedication of St Luke's Mission Church built near the junction of Stoneygate Road and Oakley Road. The Church existed here until 1947 when the successor to the earlier building was burnt down as a result of vandalism.

The 1927 Parish Church Accounts showed an addition to the electricity fund of £29-0-10d, also a donation to the Waifs and Strays Society of £4-9-4d. Expenditure included a school summer tea and a char-a-banc outing at £28-13-6d.

In 1928 electricity was installed in the church and also the Parish Room at a cost of £71-6-9d by A T Snowden Ltd. The accounts also show that a total of £47-0-0d was paid to the verger and sexton for their work over the passed twelve months. School teas in that year amounted to £12-14-0d and prizes £3-5-4d, the char-a-banc outing cost £12-12-0d. The old gas piping was sold for ten shillings. The churchwardens for that

Sunday School outing in the 1920s (LR)

year were Mr A Lathwell and H C T Bell.

The extent of Biscot's commitment to missionary work overseas, and for social work (Waifs and Strays Society) also youth work (Church Brigades) at home can be found in the 1929 Parish Church Balance Sheet. This stated that £100-18-10d was given to the above out of a total church income for that year of £339-6-3d. In that year verger and sexton fees amounted to £99-17-9d, the Sunday School teas and prizes £15-13-11d and the choir outing cost £10-10-0d.

A year after the Rev Albert Ephraim Shewring was appointed Vicar of Holy Trinity in 1930 he sent letters of appreciation to the lay readers who had helped at St Luke's Church. Negotiations were pressed forward for a Church Hall at Biscot and the following year a "Country Fair" was held in Mr Seaward's meadow to raise funds. Two marquees were booked and the fair made a profit of £76-2-10d. Land in Trinity Road was purchased for the sum of £200 and an ex-army hut obtained, which did service as the Church Institute. A matter of interest for lady members of the congregation is that Miss Edith Nears was appointed to the office of People's Warden in 1936, a position which she held for two years. A processional cross on an oak staff was purchased as a memorial to Vicar's Warden Mr A Lathwell who in 1939 had served for twenty years in this capacity. The cross is in use today.

Extracts from Biscot Parish Church Magazine December 1930

The Vicar's Letter

My Dear People,

It is with feelings of thankfulness that I am able to report the activity and co-operation of the Parochial Church Council.

In the first place, the Free Will Offering Scheme has come into being, and I hope later to add "and is a going concern". It came into operation on Advent Sunday. Those who filled in the papers and sent them to the honorary secretary, Mr F Howe, or put them in the box provided, received a bundle of 52 envelopes, one for each Sunday of the year. Each bundle of envelopes is stamped with a number, and those participating in the scheme are known only as a number ie. as number 5 or number 19 as the case may be. The envelopes are placed in the box Sunday by Sunday, and if we are away one Sunday we put in two the next, and so on. (Some are giving annually, quarterly, or monthly). Papers on which to make our promise are kept in the Church so that anyone can join the scheme at any time. The total amount of the offerings received will be published in the Magazine month by month so that we may all know how the scheme is progressing, but the persons who gave and the amount they gave will be unknown, and we shall be just numbers.

The electric light which has just been fixed in the Lych-gate is a great boon, especially on these dark nights. I am sure we appreciate it both from an aesthetic as well as from a utilitarian point of view.

The water is now laid on in the Churchyard. This I know is giving great satisfaction to the many who tend the graves of their dear ones.

At last the members of our choir are decently habited in which to lead the devotions of our people. The new cassocks and surplices have removed a grievous reproach and will enhance the importance of Divine Service.

The symbol of our salvation is now in its place over the pulpit, and a tract-case stocked with cheap but good little booklets, so helpful to those who want to know more of the religion they profess.

I would like to express my thanks to one of our sidesmen, Mr F Heard, for making us a nice substantial box with two compartments, one for the free-will offering envelopes, the other for "communications for the Vicar." The latter enables people who would like me to come and see them to put their name and address, or any other communication, in the box, which I will open each Sunday evening: it will thus create a link between your Vicar and his people, or in other words between the father and his spiritual children.

Yours sincerely   A E Shewring

Church Lads Brigade (Article from the same magazine)
We had a very fine report from the Inspecting Officer, Capt G A Anstee MC, and he congratulated us on our smartness and was very pleased to see an increase in numbers.

31st October 1930 saw the last of our recognition as a Cadet Corps. We have dispensed with our carbines and those people who so often charged us with militarism can rest assured that we are now the plain and simple Church Lads' Brigade, we are no longer cadets. Whatever action is taken by Government Departments we shall go on, and long may the C L B be the finest organisation for the elder lad; some seem to think otherwise, but like all sensible thinking citizens we are entitled to an opinion : One thing we are certain, that the C L B will grow stronger especially if we have the backing of the parents and friends.

We have made a start with the preparation for our Annual Concert. This time we are co-operating with the C G B and shall endeavour to give a "tip-top" show in February next year.

The football team is doing very well and here are the results for the month of November:

Union Chapel B B we lost by 3 goals to 2

Luton Riverdale we won by 4 goals to 2

Chapel Street Wesleyans we won by 6 goals to nil

Luton Old Modernians we won by 5 goals to nil.

The team is very fortunate in having one who is so deeply interested as Sergt Fred Gumi, and we hope that the good spirit will continue and that the League Shield will find a place at Biscot. I would appeal to our players always to play the game. *S Smith*

The Parish Magazine for 1931 will allot more space to local matter; the inset and cover will be improved. The price will be 2d. We hope for a larger circulation.

Sidesmen's Rota for December:

Dec. 7th and 28th Messrs. H C T Bell and C Stangham

Dec 14th Messrs. E Heard and E H Wilding

Dec 21st Messrs. A D Cleaver and W J Harrison

Dec 25th Messrs F E Bone and S.Smith

At the outbreak of the Second World War the Parish Room which stood between the vicarage and the stables was converted into an A R P First Aid Post. The Parish Institute which once stood in the now car park was used by the London County Council for evacuee school children. Part of the stables became a garage for ambulances and Civil Defence vehicles, the remainder converted into a school canteen

In 1956 it was decided to demolish part of the vicarage, which included the butler's pantry, the scullery, the coals and harness rooms; the Parish Room be converted into a garage for the vicar. At this time a church hall was proposed using the old school canteen and the old garage. The garage was changed into a vestibule and a porch created. A store room and toilet block was built, together with a boiler room on the side of the old garage entrance and part of the school canteen. The old school canteen was extended to include a hall stage and dressing rooms, and a separate kitchen was built. In the hall a door to the hayloft can still be seen betraying the building's original use. It would possibly have housed the stable lad. In later times it became a den for the youth club.

Youth organisations form an important part in the life of the church reaching their hey-day in the years leading up to the Second World War and after to the 1960s. At this time Holy Trinity had a company of the Church Lads Brigade, with church members playing a prominent part, Mr Howe and Mr Smith becoming leaders to the rank of Major. The Revd A Shewring often took prayers at the end of a meeting. Since then most youth organisations have shown declines, however the Brownies showed the most resilience with three packs meeting each week in the church hall up to very recent times.

During the concluding years of the Revd A E Shewring's incumbency, following the end of the war, the church was enriched by several gifts and donations, among which were a silver wafer box given in memory of Miss Higginbottom, a new Bible for the lectern as a memorial for Mrs Bull and a new cross and candlesticks for the temporary altar in the Sunday School where she had been so active. A new green frontal for the altar was given by the Little family and the congregation presented a white altar frontal, these two gifts being memorials to those who gave their lives in the Second World War. A donation of £100 was generously given by the late Mrs B Ell.

On 1st October 1955 the parish gathered to express their unanimous appreciation of the Vicar the Revd A E Shewring, who had ministered the parish of Biscot for twenty five years, and People's Warden Mr F Howe spoke on their behalf.

The Revd Shewring's successor, the Revd R C E Waller, was instituted by the Bishop of St Albans in 1956. In this year a Church Beautification fund was started, and suggestions as to how to carry out this intention at Holy Trinity Church were made by Canon Humphreys, Chairman of the Advisory Committee for Churches. The work involved continued for several years, much being done by members of the congregation, and included the cleaning of the wood and tile floors, new carpet, curtains and purple frontal, which last was given by Mrs Ozanne. Offers were received for a new chalice and other items and a larger altar cross was presented as a memorial of Peter Gilbert.

It is perhaps unfair to single out individual contributions and benefactors for there have been, and are, many who have given generously in time and money to preserve and beautify the fabric of the church which is itself but a setting for the spiritual life and social activities which characterise the parish today. In the past and at the present time, the parish has been fortunate in its clergy and lay workers who serve the community and guide its activities.

Miss E Mickleburgh, who worked tirelessly for the parish, came to Biscot in 1957 after several years on the staff of St Denys School, Murree, Pakistan and in the mid 1960s the parish had its first Lay reader, Mr K J Davies. From the mid 1950s until mid 1980s the choir was under was under the guidance of choirmaster and organist Mr C Howe, who enhanced the enjoyment of our services.

In 1956 plans for a new Church Hall, incorporating the old Parish Room and stables was drawn up. Two years later the building was officially opened by the Lady Mayor, Alderman Mrs Mary Brash. The Church Hall was refurbished in 1986. 1956 was marred, however, by the death of Mr George Seaward who had served Biscot for many years on the PCC and as Vicar's Warden. He had retired, due to ill health, in 1954 from his office as Diocesan Conference representative. In recognition of his constant concern for the welfare of others, particularly the aged and infirm, a teak seat was placed in the churchyard as a fitting memorial.

Mr Seaward had in 1958 given a Hymn and Prayer bookcase and on his death a bequest to the church was given to accrue and provide a fund to keep the Hymn and Prayer Books constantly in good repair. In 1959 an altar book was purchased in memory of the late Cyril Harrison, the cover being of goatskin leather dyed blue and ornamented with a design of cross and grapevine.

1962 was a year of great significance as plans were now put in hand for a new daughter church, St Augustine of Canterbury, to be built on the corner of Catsbrook Road and Icknield Way in Limbury. Radlett Parish offered a gift of £1,000 and a letter of grateful thanks was sent to their Vicar. It was regretfully in this same year that the Revd Richard Waller retired from the Biscot living.

The Revd Gordon Waller was instituted to the living as Vicar of Holy Trinity in 1963 by the Bishop of St Albans. His incumbency oversaw the birth of the daughter Church St Augustine of Canterbury, and saw it grow into the thriving parish of Limbury. At this time, as part of the renovation of Holy Trinity, new glass doors at the entrance to the porch were donated by Elsie Willison and her sons Roger, Colin and Peter in memory of Elsie's parents, Charles and Alice Freeman and of her husband Sidney Willison. These doors replaced the original sheep gate.

Revd Ted Bush joined the parish as assistant Curate in charge of St Augustine and worked, coaxed and bullied his parishioners, generating such enthusiasm that the forty year old hutted building from St Matthews was moved to St Augustine's site and worship commenced there. (See Chapter 16).

The foundation stone for the new Church was laid on 22nd November 1964 by the Revd John Trillo, Bishop of Bedford, and in the following months the Revd E West joined the Parish as assistant Curate and the Revd L Mayes was appointed Priest-in-Charge of St Augustine Church.

Just over twelve months after the foundation stone was laid, the very beautiful modern Church of St Augustine of Canterbury in the Parish of Limbury was consecrated by the Revd Michael Gresford Jones, Bishop of St Albans, the date being 7th December 1965. This was a very memorable and proud occasion for the Parish of Biscot, and also in a sense a humbling one, for it is a rare privilege to be participant in the erection of a building to the Glory of God.

At the annual Vestry meeting in 1966 the Vicar, Revd G H Waller explained the new procedures for the election of churchwardens; from now onwards both wardens should be chosen by the joint consent of the minister of the parish and a meeting of the parishioners. There will in future be no Vicar's warden, unless the Incumbent will not give his consent to one or the other serving as churchwarden. In this case the Incumbent appoints one warden and the other is elected by the meeting. During this year regretfully Father Ted Bush left the parish.

In 1971 the Revd Gordon H Waller left the parish to take up the living at Meppershall, and was succeeded by the Revd Eric E West who became the tenth Vicar of Biscot. The next thirty years of the Revd Eric West's incumbency was to see many changes to the ethnic make up and social life of the parish.

The church magazine "The Key" ceased publication in December 1972 after sixty years, the last copy being number 720. As well as the losses incurred over the years, its impact on the parish had lessened. In its place pamphlets and news sheets were produced to circulate throughout the parish to make it possible for more people to be aware of what is going on at Holy Trinity.

In 1974 the old vicarage was demolished; the cost of its upkeep over the years had become untenable and its size was far greater than needed in today's economic climate. The vicarage land was sold to Luton Council

Holy Trinity Vicarage (EGM)

for the building of a block of flats, the proceeds of which enabled a new vicarage to be built in the old vicarage gardens. At the same time part of the land across the road where the old institute once stood was sold off for housing, the remainder being converted into a car park for the congregation.

The large immigrant numbers coming into the parish has made it impossible to assimilate them all into our community and has resulted in separate immigrant areas. In some schools the pupil population from overseas is greater than ninety per cent.

In this climate the missionary work of the church has been very difficult, although Revd E E West has made significant inroads through his work as Christian Aid Organiser and through his contacts with young families seeking infant dedication.

The large churchyard which surrounds Holy Trinity gives the church an idyllic rural setting, but its upkeep has in the past been the cause of many a headache. Through Eric West's instigation a churchyard trust was set up with the support of the other churches in area that have former members in the churchyard. This, through donations, has enabled the grass to be cut on a regular basis together with other maintenance work, returning the churchyard to its former glory.

Miss Mickleburgh, parish worker and Mr C Howe, organist and choirmaster left Biscot in 1984. Mr E Hird took over as Organist and a new adult choir was formed with the assistance of Mr Roy Darby.

The Church Hall was refurbished in 1986 creating three walk-in store rooms and a meeting room for the PCC. The kitchen at this time was modernised with increased working surfaces and an electric oven.

In the September of 1995 the Church at Biscot made a decision to join the Forward in Faith movement, voting having taken place in December of the previous year. The Forward in Faith Movement was seen as a way ahead for the Orthodox teaching of Christian values in the Anglican Church. Holy Trinity is now under the pastoral care of the Bishop of Richborough, although in all other matters the church continues to be under the guidance of the Bishop of St Albans.

In August 1996 Miss Blanche Hook, an esteemed and well loved member of our congregation celebrated her 100th birthday with a party in the church hall which many church members attended. Sadly she died in the next February.

During the night of the 10th November 1998 extensive damage was done by vandals to the south facing stained glass windows in the nave.

These were expertly repaired and are now protected by carbon glass sheets.

Donations in memory of Hilda and Henry Jackson enabled additional heating to be installed in the church during 2002 which included a radiator in the pulpit. Concerns were expressed that this may lengthen the sermons in the winter months.

Revd Eric E West retired from the living at Biscot at the end of December 2002 and a farewell luncheon to mark the occasion was given in the Church Hall after his last service as Vicar of Holy Trinity on 29th December.

At the end of August 2004 we had the Collation of our present Vicar, Fr Thomas B Singh.

Were there nuns in Biscot? We cannot be sure, but at Holy Trinity Church there have been giants over the years, men and women who have made a difference to the life of the parish. In the 1960s and 1970s I can remember Ken and Mary Davis, Fred and Nellie Howe, Harry and Winnie Lafosse, Fred and Ida Montague, Harry Burton and Fred and Mary King, to name but a few. We stand on their shoulders today looking to the future, taking Biscot into the twenty-first century.

CHAPTER 16

Proposed New Church of St Augustine

The following is taken directly from Christian Stewardship Campaign Booklet 1961:

There are now 6,500 houses in this parish and for them all we only have our one small House of God. No wonder our parish church is overcrowded and there are many times when we need more room!

For some time discussions have been taking place between the Diocesan authorities and our own Church Council as to the best solution to this problem. An architect drew up plans for the complete reconstruction and enlargement of the parish church itself, but in view of the great development to the north of the parish it was decided first to build a daughter church which all the families centring round it could feel was very much their own.

Similar projects in many parts of the Diocese give us a guide to the estimated cost of £30,000. Normally central Diocesan funds provide the initial cost of the buildings itself and the parish furnishes and equips it.

PROPOSED NEW CHURCH OF ST AUGUSTINE

For example, the people of our neighbouring parish of St Luke's themselves produced £3,000 towards their new church.

Anything they can do we can do better – can't we?

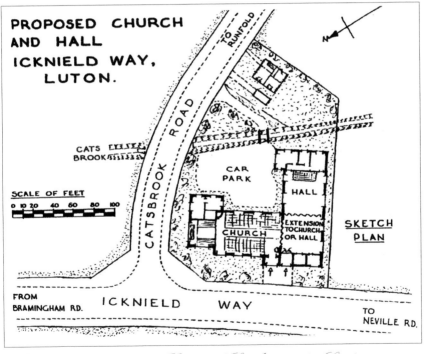

PROPOSED CHURCH AND HALL ICKNIELD WAY, LUTON.

Details of the proposed new Church of St Augustine's, Limbury (BSCB)

Interior views of St Augustine's 1968 (AH)

St Augustine's present day (CC)

Friends of Biscot Churchyard

We need your support

The churchyard is maintained by
voluntary subscriptions and donations

Please telephone Fr Thomas Singh on 01582 579410
if you would like to help

"Friends of Biscot Churchyard" is a Trust set up for the upkeep of Holy Trinity Church graveyard which is the only burial place in the Limbury-cum-Biscot area. In the past the churchyard served other churches in the area besides Anglican and the trust set up to administer the churchyard is represented from them.

If you would like to make a donation for the upkeep of the graveyard please contact Fr Thomas Singh, the Vicar of Holy Trinity Church, who will be pleased to talk to you about a one-off contribution or to make arrangements for an annual subscription if preferred.

Biscot Churchyard was laid out at the same time that the Church was built although the first burial did not take place until 1870. Originally it was approximately only half the size of the present Churchyard, the limits being marked by a line of trees on the south side. The south boundary before the enlargement was a brick wall. The enlargement was in two stages completed in 1938 from land known as Mill Common Field and today the Churchyard covers just over three acres.

All the ground to the north of the line of trees is termed Old Ground and to the south New Ground. The Churchyard is divided up into plots; plots in the Old Ground are indicated by compass readings taken from the Church. The New Ground plots use letters of the alphabet.

To help you in locating a grave we have comprehensive burial books from 1870 to the present together with a Card Index. We also have detailed maps of each plot indicating individual graves and the names of the deceased, plus books with Old Ground and New Ground grid references. In the later burial books the plot reference is given against each name helping you to locate the grave.